CS-30   GENERAL APTITUDE AND ABILITIES SERIES

This is your
PASSBOOK for...

Numerical & Alphabetical Progressions & Abstract Reasoning

Test Preparation Study Guide
Questions & Answers

COPYRIGHT NOTICE

This book is SOLELY intended for, is sold ONLY to, and its use is RESTRICTED to individual, bona fide applicants or candidates who qualify by virtue of having seriously filed applications for appropriate license, certificate, professional and/or promotional advancement, higher school matriculation, scholarship, or other legitimate requirements of education and/or governmental authorities.

This book is NOT intended for use, class instruction, tutoring, training, duplication, copying, reprinting, excerption, or adaptation, etc., by:

1) Other publishers
2) Proprietors and/or Instructors of "Coaching" and/or Preparatory Courses
3) Personnel and/or Training Divisions of commercial, industrial, and governmental organizations
4) Schools, colleges, or universities and/or their departments and staffs, including teachers and other personnel
5) Testing Agencies or Bureaus
6) Study groups which seek by the purchase of a single volume to copy and/or duplicate and/or adapt this material for use by the group as a whole without having purchased individual volumes for each of the members of the group
7) Et al.

Such persons would be in violation of appropriate Federal and State statutes.

PROVISION OF LICENSING AGREEMENTS – Recognized educational, commercial, industrial, and governmental institutions and organizations, and others legitimately engaged in educational pursuits, including training, testing, and measurement activities, may address request for a licensing agreement to the copyright owners, who will determine whether, and under what conditions, including fees and charges, the materials in this book may be used them. In other words, a licensing facility exists for the legitimate use of the material in this book on other than an individual basis. However, it is asseverated and affirmed here that the material in this book CANNOT be used without the receipt of the express permission of such a licensing agreement from the Publishers. Inquiries re licensing should be addressed to the company, attention rights and permissions department.

All rights reserved, including the right of reproduction in whole or in part, in any form or by any means, electronic or mechanical, including photocopying, recording, or by any information storage and retrieval system, without permission in writing from the Publisher.

Copyright © 2025 by
National Learning Corporation

212 Michael Drive, Syosset, NY 11791
(516) 921-8888 • www.passbooks.com
E-mail: info@passbooks.com

PASSBOOK® SERIES

THE *PASSBOOK® SERIES* has been created to prepare applicants and candidates for the ultimate academic battlefield – the examination room.

At some time in our lives, each and every one of us may be required to take an examination – for validation, matriculation, admission, qualification, registration, certification, or licensure.

Based on the assumption that every applicant or candidate has met the basic formal educational standards, has taken the required number of courses, and read the necessary texts, the *PASSBOOK® SERIES* furnishes the one special preparation which may assure passing with confidence, instead of failing with insecurity. Examination questions – together with answers – are furnished as the basic vehicle for study so that the mysteries of the examination and its compounding difficulties may be eliminated or diminished by a sure method.

This book is meant to help you pass your examination provided that you qualify and are serious in your objective.

The entire field is reviewed through the huge store of content information which is succinctly presented through a provocative and challenging approach – the question-and-answer method.

A climate of success is established by furnishing the correct answers at the end of each test.

You soon learn to recognize types of questions, forms of questions, and patterns of questioning. You may even begin to anticipate expected outcomes.

You perceive that many questions are repeated or adapted so that you can gain acute insights, which may enable you to score many sure points.

You learn how to confront new questions, or types of questions, and to attack them confidently and work out the correct answers.

You note objectives and emphases, and recognize pitfalls and dangers, so that you may make positive educational adjustments.

Moreover, you are kept fully informed in relation to new concepts, methods, practices, and directions in the field.

You discover that you are actually taking the examination all the time: you are preparing for the examination by "taking" an examination, not by reading extraneous and/or supererogatory textbooks.

In short, this PASSBOOK®, used directedly, should be an important factor in helping you to pass your test.

NUMBER AND LETTER SERIES

COMMENTARY

One of the most searching types of the arithmetic reasoning question – a basic staple of tests of general and mental ability – is the number-series problem, in which a series of single numbers (or paired numbers) is presented, which follow a certain rule or sequence. The examinee is to select the next number (or pair of numbers) if the series were to be continued in this manner.

More difficult still, and on the highest level of difficulty, is the letter-series question, wherein a series of letters, instead of numbers, is to be followed according to a definite order. Here, the element of abstractness serves to add further complexity to the problem.

Suggestion: In solving alphabetic series and progressions, it is wise to write out the alphabet and keep it in front of you. With this visual aid immediately available, the key to each series can then be solved much more easily that way.

The questions in this section test your ability to see relationships between the elements of a series. These questions are sometimes referred to as series or progressions, and, in them, the candidate is asked to determine the rule that binds the elements together and then select the following element(s) to that rule.

NUMBER SERIES/ONE NUMBER

SAMPLE QUESTIONS

DIRECTIONS: Each of the three sample questions presents a series of six numbers. Each series of numbers is made up according to a certain rule or order. You are to find what the next number in the series should be if the series were to be continued in this sequence.

1. 2 4 6 8 10 12   1._____

    A. 14   B. 16   C. 18   D. 20   E. none of these

<u>Explanation</u>

In question 1, the rule is to add 2 to each number (2 + 2 = 4; 4 + 2 = 6; etc.). The net number in the series is 14 (12 + 2 = 14). Since 14 is lettered A among the suggested answers, A is the correct answer.

2. 7 8 6 7 5 6   2._____

    A. 2   B. 3   C. 4   D. 5   E. none of these

Explanation
    In question 2, the rule is to add 1 to the first number, subtract 2 from the next, add 1, subtract 2, and so on. The next number in the series is 4; letter C is the correct answer.

3.   3 6 9 12 15 18   3.____

    A.   39   B.   40   C.   45   D.   59   E.   none of these

Explanation
    In question 3, the rule is to add 3, making 21 the next number in the series. The correct answer to question 3 is *none of these,* since 39, 40, 45 and 59 are all incorrect answers; therefore, E is the correct answer.

───────────

NUMBER SERIES PROBLEMS
COMMENTARY

Number series problems constitute an important means for measuring quantitative ability on the part of applicants for beginning and trainee positions as well as for regular, mid-level and senior level positions.

In this method, numerical reasoning forms the primary technic for measuring mathematical ability.

This test measures your ability to think with numbers instead of words.

In each problem, you are given a series of numbers that are changing according to a rule – followed by five sets of 2 numbers each. Your problem is to figure out a rule that would make one of the five sets the next two numbers in the series.

The problems do not use hard arithmetic. The task is merely to see how the numbers are related to each other. The sample questions will explain several types in detail so that you may become familiar with what you have to do.

HINTS FOR ANSWERING NUMBER SERIES QUESTIONS

1. Do the ones that are easier for you *first*. Then go back and work on the others. Enough time is allowed for you to do all the questions, provided you don't stay too long on the ones you have trouble answering.

2. Sound out the series to yourself. You may hear the rule: 2468 10 12 14 ... What are the next two numbers?

3. Look at the series carefully. You may see the rule: 9294969... What are the next two numbers?

4. If you can't hear it or see it, you may have to figure it out by writing how the numbers are changing: 6 8 16 18 26 28 36 ... What are the next two numbers?
$6+^2 8+^8 16+^2 18+^8 26+^2 36$.... What are the next two numbers if this is +2 +8? $36 + 2 = 38 + 8 = 46$ or 38 46. You would mark the letter of the answer that goes with 38 46.

5. If none of the answers given fits the rule you have figured out, try again. Try to figure out a rule that makes one of the five answers a correct one.

6. Don't spend too much time on any one question. Skip it and come back. A fresh look sometimes helps.

SAMPLE QUESTIONS

DIRECTIONS: In each of the questions in this test, there is at the top a series of numbers which follow some definite order and, below, five sets of two numbers each. You are to look at the numbers in the series at the top and find out what order they follow. Then decide what the next two numbers in that series would be if the same order were continued. Next find these two numbers in one of the sets below. *PRINT THE LETTER OF THE CORRECT ANSWER IN THE SPACE AT THE RIGHT.*

1. 1 2 3 4 5 6 7 ....   1.____

    A. 1 2   B. 5 6   C. 8 9   D. 4 5   E. 7 8

    How are these numbers changing? The numbers in this series are increasing by 1 or the rule is "add 1." If you apply this rule to the series, what would the next two numbers be? 7+1 = 8+1 = 9. Therefore, the CORRECT answer is 8 and 9, and you would select C. 8 9 as your answer.

2. 15 14 13 12 11 10 9 ....   2.____

    A. 2 1   B. 17 16   C. 8 9   D. 8 7   E. 9 8

    The numbers in this series are decreasing by 1 or the rule is to "subtract 1." If you apply that rule, what would the next two numbers be? 9-1 = 8-1 = 7. The CORRECT answer is 8 and 7, and you would select D. 8 7 as your answer.

3. 20 20 21 21 22 22 23 ....   3.____

    A. 23 23   B. 23 24   C. 19 19   D. 22 23   E. 21 22

    In this series each number is repeated and then increased by 1. The rule is to "repeat, add 1, repeat, add 1, etc." This series would be $20^{+0}20^{+1}21^{+0}21^{+1}22^{+0}22^{+1}23^{+0}23^{+1}24$. The CORRECT answer is 23 and 24, and you should have selected B. 23 24 as your answer.

4. 17 3 17 4 17 5 17 ....   4.____

    A. 6 17   B. 6 7   C. 17 6   D. 5 6   E. 17 7

    If you can't find a single rule for all the numbers in a series, see if there are really two series in the problem. This series is the number 17 separated by numbers increasing by 1, starting with 3. If the series were continued for two more numbers, it would read 17 3 17 4 17 5 17 6 17. The CORRECT answer is 6 and 17, and you should have selected A. 6 17 for question 4.

5. 1 2 4 5 7 8 10   5.____

    A. 11 12   B. 12 14   C. 10 13   D. 12 13   E. 11 13

    The rule in this series is not easy to see until you actually set down how the numbers are changing. $1^{+1}2^{+2}4^{+1}5^{+2}7^{+1}8^{+2}10$. The numbers in this series are increasing first by 1 (that is, plus 1) and then by 2 (that is, plus 2). If the series were continued for two more numbers, it would read 1 2 4 5 7 8 10 (plus 1) which is 11 (plus 2) which is 13. Therefore, the CORRECT answer is 11 and 13, and you should have selected E. 11 13 for question 5.

NOW READ AND WORK SAMPLE QUESTIONS 6 THROUGH 10 AND MARK YOUR ANSWERS IN THE SPACE PROVIDED AT THE RIGHT.

HOW TO TAKE A TEST

You have studied long, hard and conscientiously.

With your official admission card in hand, and your heart pounding, you have been admitted to the examination room.

You note that there are several hundred other applicants in the examination room waiting to take the same test.

They all appear to be equally well prepared.

You know that nothing but your best effort will suffice. The "moment of truth" is at hand: you now have to demonstrate objectively, in writing, your knowledge of content and your understanding of subject matter.

You are fighting the most important battle of your life—to pass and/or score high on an examination which will determine your career and provide the economic basis for your livelihood.

What extra, special things should you know and should you do in taking the examination?

I. YOU MUST PASS AN EXAMINATION

A. WHAT EVERY CANDIDATE SHOULD KNOW
Examination applicants often ask us for help in preparing for the written test. What can I study in advance? What kinds of questions will be asked? How will the test be given? How will the papers be graded?

B. HOW ARE EXAMS DEVELOPED?
Examinations are carefully written by trained technicians who are specialists in the field known as "psychological measurement," in consultation with recognized authorities in the field of work that the test will cover. These experts recommend the subject matter areas or skills to be tested; only those knowledges or skills important to your success on the job are included. The most reliable books and source materials available are used as references. Together, the experts and technicians judge the difficulty level of the questions.
Test technicians know how to phrase questions so that the problem is clearly stated. Their ethics do not permit "trick" or "catch" questions. Questions may have been tried out on sample groups, or subjected to statistical analysis, to determine their usefulness.
Written tests are often used in combination with performance tests, ratings of training and experience, and oral interviews. All of these measures combine to form the best-known means of finding the right person for the right job.

II. HOW TO PASS THE WRITTEN TEST

A. BASIC STEPS

1) Study the announcement

How, then, can you know what subjects to study? Our best answer is: "Learn as much as possible about the class of positions for which you've applied." The exam will test the knowledge, skills and abilities needed to do the work.

Your most valuable source of information about the position you want is the official exam announcement. This announcement lists the training and experience qualifications. Check these standards and apply only if you come reasonably close to meeting them. Many jurisdictions preview the written test in the exam announcement by including a section called "Knowledge and Abilities Required," "Scope of the Examination," or some similar heading. Here you will find out specifically what fields will be tested.

2) Choose appropriate study materials

If the position for which you are applying is technical or advanced, you will read more advanced, specialized material. If you are already familiar with the basic principles of your field, elementary textbooks would waste your time. Concentrate on advanced textbooks and technical periodicals. Think through the concepts and review difficult problems in your field.

These are all general sources. You can get more ideas on your own initiative, following these leads. For example, training manuals and publications of the government agency which employs workers in your field can be useful, particularly for technical and professional positions. A letter or visit to the government department involved may result in more specific study suggestions, and certainly will provide you with a more definite idea of the exact nature of the position you are seeking.

3) Study this book!

III. KINDS OF TESTS

Tests are used for purposes other than measuring knowledge and ability to perform specified duties. For some positions, it is equally important to test ability to make adjustments to new situations or to profit from training. In others, basic mental abilities not dependent on information are essential. Questions which test these things may not appear as pertinent to the duties of the position as those which test for knowledge and information. Yet they are often highly important parts of a fair examination. For very general questions, it is almost impossible to help you direct your study efforts. What we can do is to point out some of the more common of these general abilities needed in public service positions and describe some typical questions.

1) General information

Broad, general information has been found useful for predicting job success in some kinds of work. This is tested in a variety of ways, from vocabulary lists to questions about current events. Basic background in some field of work, such as sociology or economics, may be sampled in a group of questions. Often these are principles which have become familiar to most persons through exposure rather than through formal training. It is difficult to advise you how to study for these questions; being alert to the world around you is our best suggestion.

2) Verbal ability
An example of an ability needed in many positions is verbal or language ability. Verbal ability is, in brief, the ability to use and understand words. Vocabulary and grammar tests are typical measures of this ability. Reading comprehension or paragraph interpretation questions are common in many kinds of civil service tests. You are given a paragraph of written material and asked to find its central meaning.

IV. KINDS OF QUESTIONS

1. Multiple-choice Questions
Most popular of the short-answer questions is the "multiple choice" or "best answer" question. It can be used, for example, to test for factual knowledge, ability to solve problems or judgment in meeting situations found at work.
A multiple-choice question is normally one of three types:
- It can begin with an incomplete statement followed by several possible endings. You are to find the one ending which best completes the statement, although some of the others may not be entirely wrong.
- It can also be a complete statement in the form of a question which is answered by choosing one of the statements listed.
- It can be in the form of a problem – again you select the best answer.

Here is an example of a multiple-choice question with a discussion which should give you some clues as to the method for choosing the right answer:

When an employee has a complaint about his assignment, the action which will best help him overcome his difficulty is to
    A. discuss his difficulty with his coworkers
    B. take the problem to the head of the organization
    C. take the problem to the person who gave him the assignment
    D. say nothing to anyone about his complaint

In answering this question, you should study each of the choices to find which is best. Consider choice "A" – Certainly an employee may discuss his complaint with fellow employees, but no change or improvement can result, and the complaint remains unresolved. Choice "B" is a poor choice since the head of the organization probably does not know what assignment you have been given, and taking your problem to him is known as "going over the head" of the supervisor. The supervisor, or person who made the assignment, is the person who can clarify it or correct any injustice. Choice "C" is, therefore, correct. To say nothing, as in choice "D," is unwise. Supervisors have and interest in knowing the problems employees are facing, and the employee is seeking a solution to his problem.

2. True/False

3. Matching Questions
Matching an answer from a column of choices within another column.

V. RECORDING YOUR ANSWERS

Computer terminals are used more and more today for many different kinds of exams.

For an examination with very few applicants, you may be told to record your answers in the test booklet itself. Separate answer sheets are much more common. If this separate answer sheet is to be scored by machine – and this is often the case – it is highly important that you mark your answers correctly in order to get credit.

VI. BEFORE THE TEST

YOUR PHYSICAL CONDITION IS IMPORTANT

If you are not well, you can't do your best work on tests. If you are half asleep, you can't do your best either. Here are some tips:

1) Get about the same amount of sleep you usually get. Don't stay up all night before the test, either partying or worrying—DON'T DO IT!
2) If you wear glasses, be sure to wear them when you go to take the test. This goes for hearing aids, too.
3) If you have any physical problems that may keep you from doing your best, be sure to tell the person giving the test. If you are sick or in poor health, you relay cannot do your best on any test. You can always come back and take the test some other time.

Common sense will help you find procedures to follow to get ready for an examination. Too many of us, however, overlook these sensible measures. Indeed, nervousness and fatigue have been found to be the most serious reasons why applicants fail to do their best on civil service tests. Here is a list of reminders:

- Begin your preparation early – Don't wait until the last minute to go scurrying around for books and materials or to find out what the position is all about.
- Prepare continuously – An hour a night for a week is better than an all-night cram session. This has been definitely established. What is more, a night a week for a month will return better dividends than crowding your study into a shorter period of time.
- Locate the place of the exam – You have been sent a notice telling you when and where to report for the examination. If the location is in a different town or otherwise unfamiliar to you, it would be well to inquire the best route and learn something about the building.
- Relax the night before the test – Allow your mind to rest. Do not study at all that night. Plan some mild recreation or diversion; then go to bed early and get a good night's sleep.
- Get up early enough to make a leisurely trip to the place for the test – This way unforeseen events, traffic snarls, unfamiliar buildings, etc. will not upset you.
- Dress comfortably – A written test is not a fashion show. You will be known by number and not by name, so wear something comfortable.
- Leave excess paraphernalia at home – Shopping bags and odd bundles will get in your way. You need bring only the items mentioned in the official notice you received; usually everything you need is provided. Do not bring reference books to the exam. They will only confuse those last minutes and be taken away from you when in the test room.

- Arrive somewhat ahead of time – If because of transportation schedules you must get there very early, bring a newspaper or magazine to take your mind off yourself while waiting.
- Locate the examination room – When you have found the proper room, you will be directed to the seat or part of the room where you will sit. Sometimes you are given a sheet of instructions to read while you are waiting. Do not fill out any forms until you are told to do so; just read them and be prepared.
- Relax and prepare to listen to the instructions
- If you have any physical problem that may keep you from doing your best, be sure to tell the test administrator. If you are sick or in poor health, you really cannot do your best on the exam. You can come back and take the test some other time.

VII. AT THE TEST

The day of the test is here and you have the test booklet in your hand. The temptation to get going is very strong. Caution! There is more to success than knowing the right answers. You must know how to identify your papers and understand variations in the type of short-answer question used in this particular examination. Follow these suggestions for maximum results from your efforts:

1) Cooperate with the monitor

The test administrator has a duty to create a situation in which you can be as much at ease as possible. He will give instructions, tell you when to begin, check to see that you are marking your answer sheet correctly, and so on. He is not there to guard you, although he will see that your competitors do not take unfair advantage. He wants to help you do your best.

2) Listen to all instructions

Don't jump the gun! Wait until you understand all directions. In most civil service tests you get more time than you need to answer the questions. So don't be in a hurry. Read each word of instructions until you clearly understand the meaning. Study the examples, listen to all announcements and follow directions. Ask questions if you do not understand what to do.

3) Identify your papers

Civil service exams are usually identified by number only. You will be assigned a number; you must not put your name on your test papers. Be sure to copy your number correctly. Since more than one exam may be given, copy your exact examination title.

4) Plan your time

Unless you are told that a test is a "speed" or "rate of work" test, speed itself is usually not important. Time enough to answer all the questions will be provided, but this does not mean that you have all day. An overall time limit has been set. Divide the total time (in minutes) by the number of questions to determine the approximate time you have for each question.

5) Do not linger over difficult questions

If you come across a difficult question, mark it with a paper clip (useful to have along) and come back to it when you have been through the booklet. One caution if you do this – be sure to skip a number on your answer sheet as well. Check often to be sure that you have not lost your place and that you are marking in the row numbered the same as the question you are answering.

6) Read the questions

Be sure you know what the question asks! Many capable people are unsuccessful because they failed to read the questions correctly.

7) Answer all questions

Unless you have been instructed that a penalty will be deducted for incorrect answers, it is better to guess than to omit a question.

8) Speed tests

It is often better NOT to guess on speed tests. It has been found that on timed tests people are tempted to spend the last few seconds before time is called in marking answers at random – without even reading them – in the hope of picking up a few extra points. To discourage this practice, the instructions may warn you that your score will be "corrected" for guessing. That is, a penalty will be applied. The incorrect answers will be deducted from the correct ones, or some other penalty formula will be used.

9) Review your answers

If you finish before time is called, go back to the questions you guessed or omitted to give them further thought. Review other answers if you have time.

10) Return your test materials

If you are ready to leave before others have finished or time is called, take ALL your materials to the monitor and leave quietly. Never take any test material with you. The monitor can discover whose papers are not complete, and taking a test booklet may be grounds for disqualification.

VIII. EXAMINATION TECHNIQUES

1) Read the general instructions carefully. These are usually printed on the first page of the exam booklet. As a rule, these instructions refer to the timing of the examination; the fact that you should not start work until the signal and must stop work at a signal, etc. If there are any special instructions, such as a choice of questions to be answered, make sure that you note this instruction carefully.

2) When you are ready to start work on the examination, that is as soon as the signal has been given, read the instructions to each question booklet, underline any key words or phrases, such as least, best, outline, describe and the like. In this way you will tend to answer as requested rather than discover on reviewing your paper that you listed without describing, that you selected the worst choice rather than the best choice, etc.

3) If the examination is of the objective or multiple-choice type – that is, each question will also give a series of possible answers: A, B, C or D, and you are called upon to select the best answer and write the letter next to that answer on your answer paper – it is advisable to start answering each question in turn. There may be anywhere from 50 to 100 such questions in the three or four hours allotted and you can see how much time would be taken if you read through all the questions before beginning to answer any. Furthermore, if you

come across a question or group of questions which you know would be difficult to answer, it would undoubtedly affect your handling of all the other questions.

4) If the examination is of the essay type and contains but a few questions, it is a moot point as to whether you should read all the questions before starting to answer any one. Of course, if you are given a choice – say five out of seven and the like – then it is essential to read all the questions so you can eliminate the two that are most difficult. If, however, you are asked to answer all the questions, there may be danger in trying to answer the easiest one first because you may find that you will spend too much time on it. The best technique is to answer the first question, then proceed to the second, etc.

5) Time your answers. Before the exam begins, write down the time it started, then add the time allowed for the examination and write down the time it must be completed, then divide the time available somewhat as follows:
   - If 3-1/2 hours are allowed, that would be 210 minutes. If you have 80 objective-type questions, that would be an average of 2-1/2 minutes per question. Allow yourself no more than 2 minutes per question, or a total of 160 minutes, which will permit about 50 minutes to review.
   - If for the time allotment of 210 minutes there are 7 essay questions to answer, that would average about 30 minutes a question. Give yourself only 25 minutes per question so that you have about 35 minutes to review.

6) The most important instruction is to read each question and make sure you know what is wanted. The second most important instruction is to time yourself properly so that you answer every question. The third most important instruction is to answer every question. Guess if you have to but include something for each question. Remember that you will receive no credit for a blank and will probably receive some credit if you write something in answer to an essay question. If you guess a letter – say "B" for a multiple-choice question – you may have guessed right. If you leave a blank as an answer to a multiple-choice question, the examiners may respect your feelings but it will not add a point to your score. Some exams may penalize you for wrong answers, so in such cases only, you may not want to guess unless you have some basis for your answer.

7) Suggestions
   a. Objective-type questions
      1. Examine the question booklet for proper sequence of pages and questions
      2. Read all instructions carefully
      3. Skip any question which seems too difficult; return to it after all other questions have been answered
      4. Apportion your time properly; do not spend too much time on any single question or group of questions
      5. Note and underline key words – all, most, fewest, least, best, worst, same, opposite, etc.
      6. Pay particular attention to negatives
      7. Note unusual option, e.g., unduly long, short, complex, different or similar in content to the body of the question
      8. Observe the use of "hedging" words – probably, may, most likely, etc.

9. Make sure that your answer is put next to the same number as the question
10. Do not second-guess unless you have good reason to believe the second answer is definitely more correct
11. Cross out original answer if you decide another answer is more accurate; do not erase until you are ready to hand your paper in
12. Answer all questions; guess unless instructed otherwise
13. Leave time for review

b. Essay questions
1. Read each question carefully
2. Determine exactly what is wanted. Underline key words or phrases.
3. Decide on outline or paragraph answer
4. Include many different points and elements unless asked to develop any one or two points or elements
5. Show impartiality by giving pros and cons unless directed to select one side only
6. Make and write down any assumptions you find necessary to answer the questions
7. Watch your English, grammar, punctuation and choice of words
8. Time your answers; don't crowd material

8) Answering the essay question

Most essay questions can be answered by framing the specific response around several key words or ideas. Here are a few such key words or ideas:

M's: manpower, materials, methods, money, management
P's: purpose, program, policy, plan, procedure, practice, problems, pitfalls, personnel, public relations

a. Six basic steps in handling problems:
1. Preliminary plan and background development
2. Collect information, data and facts
3. Analyze and interpret information, data and facts
4. Analyze and develop solutions as well as make recommendations
5. Prepare report and sell recommendations
6. Install recommendations and follow up effectiveness

b. Pitfalls to avoid
1. Taking things for granted – A statement of the situation does not necessarily imply that each of the elements is necessarily true; for example, a complaint may be invalid and biased so that all that can be taken for granted is that a complaint has been registered
2. Considering only one side of a situation – Wherever possible, indicate several alternatives and then point out the reasons you selected the best one
3. Failing to indicate follow up – Whenever your answer indicates action on your part, make certain that you will take proper follow-up action to see how successful your recommendations, procedures or actions turn out to be
4. Taking too long in answering any single question – Remember to time your answers properly

EXAMINATION SECTION

NUMBER SERIES PROBLEMS
COMMENTARY

Number series problems constitute an important means for measuring quantitative ability on the part of applicants for beginning and trainee positions as well as for regular, mid-level, and senior level positions.

In this method, numerical reasoning forms the primary technic for measuring mathematic-cal ability.

This test measures your ability to think with numbers instead of words.

In each problem, you are given a series of numbers that are changing according to a rule - followed by five sets of 2 numbers each. Your problem is to figure out a rule that would make one of the five sets the next two numbers in the series.

The problems do not use hard arithmetic. The task is merely to see how the numbers are related to each other. The sample questions will explain several types in detail so that you may become familiar with what you have to do.

HINTS FOR ANSWERING NUMBER SERIES QUESTIONS

1. Do the ones that are easier for you *first*. Then go back and work on the others. Enough time is allowed for you to do all the questions, provided you don't stay too long on the ones you have trouble answering.
2. Sound out the series to yourself. You may hear the rule: 2468 10 12 14 ... What are the next two numbers?
3. Look at the series carefully. You may see the rule: 9294969... What are the next two numbers?
4. If you can't hear it or see it, you may have to figure it out by writing down how the numbers are changing: 6 8 16 18 26 28 36 ... What are the next two numbers?
   6^{+2} 8^{+8} 16^{+2} 18^{+8} 26^{+2} 28^{+8} 36.... What are the next two numbers if this is +2 +8? 36 + 2 = 38 + 8 = 46 or 38 46. You would mark the letter of the answer that goes with 38 46.
5. If none of the answers given fits the rule you have figured out, try again. Try to figure out a rule that makes one of the five answers a correct one.
6. Don't spend too much time on any one question. Skip it and come back. A fresh look sometimes helps.

SAMPLE QUESTIONS

DIRECTIONS: In each of the questions in this test, there is at the top a series of numbers which follow some definite order and, below, five sets of two numbers each. You are to look at the numbers in the series at the top and find out what order they follow. Then decide what the next two numbers in that series would be if the same order were continued. Next find these two numbers in one of the sets below. *PRINT THE LETTER OF THE CORRECT ANSWER IN THE SPACE AT THE RIGHT.*

1. 1 2 3 4 5 6 7 .....

   A. 1 2   B. 5 6   C. 8 9   D. 4 5   E. 7 8

   How are these numbers changing? The numbers in this series are increasing by 1 or the rule is "add 1." If you apply this rule to the series, what would the next two numbers be? 7+1=8+1=9.
   Therefore, the CORRECT answer is 8 and 9, and you would select C. 8 9 as your answer.

2. 15 14 13 12 11 10 9 ....

   A. 2 1   B. 17 16   C. 8 9   D. 8 7   E. 9 8

   The numbers in this series are decreasing by 1 or the rule is "subtract 1." If you apply that rule, what would the next two numbers be? 9-1=8-1=7. The CORRECT answer is 8 and 7, and you would select D. 8 7 as your answer.

3. 20 20 21 21 22 22 23 ....

   A. 23 23   B. 23 24   C. 19 19   D. 22 23   E. 21 22

   In this series each number is repeated and then increased by 1. The rule is "repeat, add 1, repeat, add 1, etc." The series would be $20^{+0}20^{+1}21^{+0}21^{+1}22^{+0}22^{+1}23^{+0}23^{+1}24$. The CORRECT answer is 23 and 24, and you should have selected B. 23 24 as your answer.

4. 17 3 17 4 17 5 17 ....

   A. 6 17   B. 6 7   C. 17 6   D. 5 6   E. 17 7

   If you can't find a single rule for all the numbers in a series, see if there are really two series in the problem. This series is the number 17 separated by numbers increasing by 1, starting with 3. If the series were continued for two more numbers, it would read 17 3 17 4 17 5 17 6 17. The CORRECT answer is 6 and 17, and you should have selected A. 6 17 for question 4.

5. 1 2 4 5 7 8 10 ....

   A. 11 12   B. 12 14   C. 10 13   D. 12 13   E. 11 13

   The rule in this series is not easy to see until you actually set down how the numbers are changing: $1^{+1}2^{+2}4^{+1}5^{+2}7^{+1}8^{+2}10$. The numbers in this series are increasing first by 1 (that is, plus 1) and then by 2 (that is, plus 2). If the series were continued for two more numbers, it would read: 1 2 4 5 7 8 10 (plus 1) which is 11 (plus 2) which is 13. Therefore, the CORRECT answer is 11 and 13, and you should have selected E. 11 13 for question 5.

NOW READ AND WORK SAMPLE QUESTIONS 6 THROUGH 10 AND MARK FOUR ANSWERS IN THE SPACE PROVIDED AT THE RIGHT.

6. 21 21 20 20 19 19 18 ....
    A. 18 18   B. 18 17   C. 17 18   D. 17 17   E. 18 19

7. 1 22 1 23 1 24 1 ....
    A. 2 61   B. 25 26   C. 2 51   D. 1 26   E. 1 25

8. 1 20 3 19 5 18 7 ....
    A. 8 9   B. 8 17   C. 17 10   D. 17 9   E. 9 18

9. 4 7 10 13 16 19 22 ...
    A. 23 26   B. 25 27   C. 25 26   D. 25 28   E. 24 27

10. 30 2 28 4 26 6 24 ....
    A. 23 9   B. 26 8   C. 8 9   D. 26 22   E. 8 22

EXPLANATIONS FOR QUESTIONS 6 THROUGH 10.

6. Each number in the series repeats itself and then decreases by 1 or minus 1; 21 (repeat) 21 (minus 1) which makes 20 (repeat) 20 (minus 1) which makes 19 (repeat) 19 (minus 1) which makes 18 (repeat) ? (minus 1) ? The CORRECT answer is B.

7. The number 1 is separated by numbers which begin with 22 and increase by 1; 1 22 1 (increase 22 by 1) which makes 23 1 (increase 23 by 1) which makes 24 1 (increase 24 by 1) which makes ? The CORRECT answer is C.

8. This is best explained by two alternating series - one series starts with 1 and increases by 2 or plus 2; the other series starts with 20 and decreases by 1 or minus 1. The CORRECT answer is D.

$$1\uparrow 3\uparrow 5\uparrow 7\uparrow ?$$

9. This series of numbers increases by 3 (plus 3) beginning with the first number - 4 (plus 3) 7 (plus 3) 10 (plus 3) 13 (plus 3) 16 (plus 3) 19 (plus 3) 22 (plus 3) ? The CORRECT answer is D.

10. Look for two alternating series - one series starts with 30 and decreases by 2 (minus 2); the other series starts with 2 and increases by 2 (plus 2). The CORRECT answer is E.

$$30\uparrow 28\uparrow 26\uparrow 24\uparrow ?$$
$$2\quad 4\quad 6\quad 7$$

KEY (CORRECT ANSWERS)

1.	C		6.	B
2.	D		7.	C
3.	B		8.	D
4.	A		9.	D
5.	E		10.	E

NUMBER SERIES PROBLEMS
EXAMINATION SECTION
TEST 1

DIRECTIONS: In each of the questions in this test, there is at the top a series of numbers which follow some definite order and, below, five sets of two numbers each. You are to look at the numbers in the series at the top and find out what order they follow. Then decide what the next two numbers in that series would be if the same order were continued. Next find these two numbers in one of the sets below. *PRINT THE LETTER OF THE CORRECT ANSWER IN THE SPACE AT THE RIGHT.*

1. 5 6 20 7 8 19 9 ....   1.___
   A. 10 18   B. 18 17   C. 10 17   D. 18 19   E. 10 11

2. 9 10 1 11 12 2 13 ....   2.___
   A. 2 14   B. 3 14   C. 14 3   D. 14 15   E. 14 1

3. 4 6 9 11 14 16 19 ....   3.___
   A. 21 24   B. 22 25   C. 20 22   D. 21 23   E. 22 24

4. 8 8 1 10 10 3 12 ....   4.___
   A. 13 13   B. 12 5   C. 12 4   D. 13 5   E. 4 12

5. 14 1 2 15 3 4 16 ....   5.___
   A. 5 16   B. 6 7   C. 5 17   D. 5 6   E. 17 5

6. 10 12 50 15 17 50 20 ....   6.___
   A. 50 21   B. 21 50   C. 50 22   D. 22 50   E. 22 24

7. 1 2 3 50 4 5 6 51 7 8 ....   7.___
   A. 9 10   B. 9 52   C. 51 10   D. 10 52   E. 10 50

8. 20 21 23 24 27 28 32 33 38 39 ....   8.___
   A. 45 46   B. 45 52   C. 44 45   D. 44 49   E. 40 46

9. 17 15 21 18 10 16 19 ....   9.___
   A. 20 5   B. 5 11   C. 11 11   D. 11 20   E. 15 14

10. 12 16 10 14 8 12 6 ....   10.___
    A. 10 14   B. 10 8   C. 10 4   D. 4 10   E. 4 2

KEY (CORRECT ANSWERS)

1.	A	6.	D
2.	C	7.	B
3.	A	8.	A
4.	B	9.	B
5.	D	10.	C

TEST 2

DIRECTIONS: In each of the questions in this test, there is at the top a series of numbers which follow some definite order and, below, five sets of two numbers each. You are to look at the numbers in the series at the top and find out what order they follow. Then decide what the next two numbers in that series would be if the same order were continued. Next find these two numbers in one of the sets below. *PRINT THE LETTER OF THE CORRECT ANSWER IN THE SPACE AT THE RIGHT.*

1. 10 11 12 10 11 12 10 ....   1.____
   A. 10 13   B. 12 10   C. 11 10   D. 11 12   E. 10 12

2. 4 6 7 4 6 7 4   2.____
   A. .6 7   B. 4 7   C. 7 6   D. 7 4   E. 6 8

3. 7 7 3 7 7 4 7 ....   3.____
   A. 4 5   B. 4 7   C. 5 7   D. 7 5   E. 7 7

4. 3 4 10 5 6 10 7 ....   4.____
   A. 10 8   B. 9 8   C. 8 14   D. 8 9   E. 8 10

5. 6 6 7 7 8 8 9 ....   5.____
   A. 10 11   B. 10 10   C. 9 10   D. 9 9   E. 10 9

6. 3 8 9 4 9 10 5 ....   6.____
   A. 6 10   B. 10 11   C. 9 10   D. 11 6   E. 10 6

7. 2 4 3 6 4 8 5 ....   7.____
   A. 6 10   B. 10 7   C. 10 6   D. 9 6   E. 6 7

8. 11 5 9 7 7 9 5 ....   8.____
   A. 11 3   B. 7 9   C. 7 11   D. 9 7   E. 3 7

9. 12 10 8 8 6 4 4 ....   9.____
   A. 2 2   B. 6 4   C. 6 2   D. 4 6   E. 2 0

10. 20 22 22 19 21 21 18 ....   10.____
    A. 22 22   B. 19 19   C. 20 20   D. 20 17   E. 19 17

KEY (CORRECT ANSWERS)

1. D   6. B
2. A   7. C
3. D   8. A
4. E   9. E
5. C   10. C

TEST 3

DIRECTIONS: In each of the questions in this test, there is at the top a series of numbers which follow some definite order and, below, five sets of two numbers each. You are to look at the numbers in the series at the top and find out what order they follow. Then decide what the next two numbers in that series would be if the same order were continued. Next find these two numbers in one of the sets below. *PRINT THE LETTER OF THE CORRECT ANSWER IN THE SPACE AT THE RIGHT.*

1. 5 7 6 10 7 13 8 ....
    A. 16 9   B. 16 10   C. 9 15   D. 10 15   E. 15 9   1.____

2. 13 10 11 15 12 13 17 ....
    A. 18 14   B. 18 15   C. 15 16   D. 14 15   E. 15 18   2.____

3. 30 27 24 21 18 15 12 ....
    A. 9 3   B. 9 6   C. 6 3   D. 12 9   E. 8 5   3.____

4. 3 7 10 5 8 10 7 ....
    A. 10 11   B. 10 5   C. 10 9   D. 10 10   E. 9 10   4.____

5. 12 4 13 6 14 8 15 ....
    A. 10 17   B. 17 10   C. 10 12   D. 16 10   E. 10 16   5.____

6. 21 8 18 20 7 17 19 ....
    A. 16 18   B. 18 6   C. 6 16   D. 5 15   E. 6 18   6.____

7. 14 16 16 18 20 20 22 ....
    A. 22 24   B. 26 28   C. 24 26   D. 24 24   E. 24 28   7.____

8. 5 6 8 9 12 13 17 ....
    A. 18 23   B. 13 18   C. 18 22   D. 23 24   E. 18 19   8.____

9. 1 3 5 5 2 4 6 6 3 ....
    A. 7 4   B. 5 5   C. 1 3   D. 5 7   E. 7 7   9.____

10. 12 24 15 25 18 26 21 ....
    A. 27 22   B. 24 22   C. 29 24   D. 27 27   E. 27 24   10.____

KEY (CORRECT ANSWERS)

1. A   6. C
2. D   7. D
3. B   8. A
4. E   9. D
5. E   10. E

TEST 4

DIRECTIONS: In each of the questions in this test, there is at the top a series of numbers which follow some definite order and, below, five sets of two numbers each. You are to look at the numbers in the series at the top and find out what order they follow. Then decide what the next two numbers in that series would be if the same order were continued. Next find these two numbers in one of the sets below. *PRINT THE LETTER OF THE CORRECT ANSWER IN THE SPACE AT THE RIGHT.*

1. 8 9 9 8 10 10 8 ....
    A. 11 8   B. 8 13   C. 8 11   D. 11 11   E. 8 8
    1.____

2. 10 10 11 11 12 12 13 ....
    A. 15 15   B. 13 13   C. 14 14   D. 13 14   E. 14 15
    2.____

3. 6 6 10 6 6 12 6 ....
    A. 6 14   B. 13 6   C. 14 6   D. 6 13   E. 6 6
    3.____

4. 17 11 5 16 10 4 15 ....
    A. 13 9   B. 13 11   C. 8 5   D. 9 5   E. 9 3
    4.____

5. 1 3 2 4 3 5 4 ....
    A. 6 8   B. 5 6   C. 6 5   D. 3 4   E. 3 5
    5.____

6. 11 11 10 12 12 11 13 ....
    A. 12 14   B. 14 12   C. 14 14   D. 13 14   E. 13 12
    6.____

7. 18 5 6 18 7 8 18 ....
    A. 9 9   B. 9 10   C. 18 9   D. 8 9   E. 18 7
    7.____

8. 7 8 9 13 10 11 12 14 13 14 ....
    A. 15 16   B. 13 15   C. 14 15   D. 15 15   E. 13 14
    8.____

9. 5 7 30 9 11 30 13 ....
    A. 15 16   B. 15 17   C. 14 17   D. 15 30   E. 30 17
    9.____

10. 5 7 11 13 17 19 23 ....
    A. 27 29   B. 25 29   C. 25 27   D. 27 31   E. 29 31
    10.____

KEY (CORRECT ANSWERS)

1. D   6. E
2. D   7. B
3. A   8. D
4. E   9. D
5. C   10. B

TEST 5

DIRECTIONS: In each of the questions in this test, there is at the top a series of numbers which follow some definite order and, below, five sets of two numbers each. You are to look at the numbers in the series at the top and find out what order they follow. Then decide what the next two numbers in that series would be if the same order were continued. Next find these two numbers in one of the sets below. *PRINT THE LETTER OF THE CORRECT ANSWER IN THE SPACE AT THE RIGHT.*

1. 9 15 10 17 12 19 15 21 19 ....
   A. 23 24   B. 25 23   C. 17 23   D. 23 31   E. 21 24   1.____

2. 34 37 30 33 26 29 22 ....
   A. 17 8   B. 18 11   C. 25 28   D. 25 20   E. 25 18   2.____

3. 10 16 12 14 14 12 16 ....
   A. 14 12   B. 10 18   C. 10 14   D. 14 18   E. 14 16   3.____

4. 11 12 18 11 13 19 11 14 ....
   A. 18 11   B. 16 11   C. 20 11   D. 11 21   E. 17 11   4.____

5. 20 9 8 19 10 9 18 11 10 ....
   A. 19 11   B. 17 10   C. 19 12   D. 17 12   E. 19 10   5.____

6. 28 27 26 31 30 29 34 ....
   A. 36 32   B. 32 31   C. 33 32   D. 33 36   E. 35 36   6.____

7. 10 16 14 20 18 24 22 ....
   A. 28 32   B. 27 26   C. 28 26   D. 26 28   E. 27 28   7.____

8. 9 9 7 8 7 7 9 10 5 ....
   A. 5 11   B. 11 12   C. 5 9   D. 9 11   E. 5 5   8.____

9. 5 7 11 17 10 12 16 22 15 17 ....
   A. 27 26   B. 19 23   C. 19 27   D. 21 23   E. 21 27   9.____

10. 12 19 13 20 14 21 15 ....
   A. 16 17   B. 22 16   C. 16 22   D. 15 22   E. 15 16   10.____

KEY (CORRECT ANSWERS)

6. A   11. C
7. E   12. C
8. B   13. A
9. C   14. E
10. D   15. B

TEST 6

DIRECTIONS : In each of the questions in this test, there is at the top a series of numbers which follow some definite order and, below, five sets of two numbers each. You are to look at the numbers in the series at the top and find out what order they follow. Then decide what the next two numbers in that series would be if the same order were continued. Next find these two numbers in one of the sets below. *PRINT THE LETTER OF THE CORRECT ANSWER IN THE SPACE AT THE RIGHT.*

1. 13 12 8 11 10 8 9 ....   1.____
   A. 8 7   B. 6 8   C. 8 6   D. 8 8   E. 7 8

2. 13 18 13 17 13 16 13 ....   2.____
   A. 15 13   B. 13 14   C. 13 15   D. 14 15   E. 15 14

3. 13 13 10 12 12 10 11 ....   3.____
   A. 10 10   B. 10 9   C. 11 9   D. 9 11   E. 11 10

4. 6 5 4 6 5 4 6 ....   4.____
   A. 4 6   B. 6 4   C. 5 4   D. 5 6   E. 4 5

5. 10 10 9 8 8 7 6 ....   5.____
   A. 5 5   B. 5 4   C. 6 5   D. 6 4   E. 5 3

6. 20 16 18 14 16 12 14 ....   6.____
   A. 16 12   B. 10 12   C. 16 18   D. 12 12   E. 12 10

7. 7 12 8 11 9 10 10 ....   7.____
   A. 11 9   B. 9 8   C. 9 11   D. 10 11   E. 9 10

8. 13 13 12 15 15 14 17 ....   8.____
   A. 17 16   B. 14 17   C. 16 19   D. 19 19   E. 16 16

9. 19 18 12 17 16 13 15 ....   9.____
   A. 16 12   B. 14 14   C. 12 14   D. 14 12   E. 12 16

10. 7 15 12 8 16 13 9 ....   10.____
    A. 17 14   B. 17 10   C. 14 10   D. 14 17   E. 10 14

KEY (CORRECT ANSWERS)

1. D   6. B
2. A   7. C
3. E   8. A
4. C   9. B
5. C   10. A

TEST 7

DIRECTIONS: In each of the questions in this test, there is at the top a series of numbers which follow some definite order and, below, five sets of two numbers each. You are to look at the numbers in the series at the top and find out what order they follow. Then decide what the next two numbers in that series would be if the same order were continued. Next find these two numbers in one of the sets below. *PRINT THE LETTER OF THE CORRECT ANSWER IN THE SPACE AT THE RIGHT.*

1. 18 15 6 16 14 6 14 ....
   A. 12 6   B. 14 13   C. 6 12   D. 13 12   E. 13 6   1.___

2. 6 6 5 8 8 7 10 10 ....
   A. 8 12   B. 9 12   C. 12 12   D. 12 9   E. 9 9   2.___

3. 17 20 23 26 29 32 35 ....
   A. 37 40   B. 41 44   C. 38 41   D. 38 42   E. 36 39   3.___

4. 15 5 7 16 9 11 17 ....
   A. 18 13   B. 15 17   C. 12 19   D. 13 15   E. 12 13   4.___

5. 19 17 16 16 13 15 10 ....
   A. 14 7   B. 12 9   C. 14 9   D. 7 12   E. 10 14   5.___

6. 11 1 16 10 6 21 9 ....
   A. 12 26   B. 26 8   C. 11 26   D. 11 8   E. 8 11   6.___

7. 21 21 19 17 17 15 13 ....
   A. 11 11   B. 13 11   C. 11 9   D. 9 7   E. 13 13   7.___

8. 23 22 20 19 16 15 11 ....
   A. 6 5   B. 10 9   C. 6 1   D. 10 6   E. 10 5   8.___

9. 17 10 16 9 14 8 11 ....
   A. 7 11   B. 7 7   C. 10 4   D. 4 10   E. 7 4   9.___

10. 11 9 14 12 17 15 20 18 23 ....
    A. 21 24   B. 26 21   C. 21 26   D. 24 27   E. 26 29   10.___

KEY (CORRECT ANSWERS)

1. E   6. C
2. B   7. B
3. C   8. E
4. D   9. B
5. A   10. C

TEST 8

DIRECTIONS : In each of the questions in this test, there is at the top a series of numbers which follow some definite order and, below, five sets of two numbers each. You are to look at the numbers in the series at the top and find out what order they follow. Then decide what the next two numbers in that series would be if the same order were continued. Next find these two numbers in one of the sets below. *PRINT THE LETTER OF THE CORRECT ANSWER IN THE SPACE AT THE RIGHT.*

1. 13 4 5 13 6 7 13 ....   1.____
   A. 13 8   B. 8 13   C. 8 9   D. 8 8   E. 7 8

2. 10 10 9 11 11 10 12 ....   2.____
   A. 13 14   B. 12 11   C. 13 13   D. 12 12   E. 12 13

3. 6 6 8 10 10 12 14 ....   3.____
   A. 14 14   B. 14 16   C. 16 16   D. 12 14   E. 10 10

4. 8 1 9 3 10 5 11 ....   4.____
   A. 7 12   B. 6 12   C. 12 6   D. 7 8   E. 6 7

5. 30 11 24 12 19 14 15 17 12 21 10 ....   5.____
   A. 23 8   B. 25 8   C. 26 9   D. 24 9   E. 25 9

6. 24 30 29 22 28 27 19 26 25 15 24 ....   6.____
   A. 14 23   B. 19 18   C. 23 22   D. 25 11   E. 23 10

7. 7 5 9 7 11 9 13 ....   7.____
   A. 11 14   B. 10 15   C. 11 15   D. 12 14   E. 10 14

8. 9 10 11 7 8 9 5 ....   8.____
   A. 6 7   B. 7 8   C. 5 6   D. 6 4   E. 7 5

9. 8 9 10 10 9 10 11 11 10 11 12 ....   9.____
   A. 11 12   B. 12 10   C. 11 11   D. 12 11   E. 11 13

10. 5 6 8 9 12 13 17 18 23 24 ....   10.____
    A. 30 31   B. 25 31   C. 29 30   D. 25 30   E. 30 37

KEY (CORRECT ANSWERS)

1. C
2. B
3. B
4. A
5. C

6. E
7. C
8. A
9. D
10. A

TEST 9

DIRECTIONS: In each of the questions in this test, there is at the top a series of numbers which follow some definite order and, below, five sets of two numbers each. You are to look at the numbers in the series at the top and find out what order they follow. Then decide what the next two numbers in that series would be if the same order were continued. Next find these two numbers in one of the sets below. PRINT THE LETTER OF THE CORRECT ANSWER IN THE SPACE AT THE RIGHT.

1. 8 9 10 8 9 10 8 ....   1.____
   A. 8 9   B. 9 10   C. 9 8   D. 10 8   E. 8 10

2. 3 4 4 3 5 5 3 ....   2.____
   A. 3 3   B. 6 3   C. 3 6   D. 6 6   E. 6 7

3. 7 7 3 7 7 4 7 ....   3.____
   A. 7 7   B. 7 8   C. 5 7   D. 8 7   E. 7 5

4. 18 18 19 20 20 21 22 ....   4.____
   A. 22 23   B. 23 24   C. 23 23   D. 22 22   E. 21 22

5. 2 6 10 3 7 11 4 ....   5.____
   A. 12 16   B. 5 9   C. 8 5   D. 12 5   E. 8 12

6. 11 8 15 12 19 16 23 ....   6.____
   A. 27 20   B. 24 20   C. 27 24   D. 20 24   E. 20 27

7. 16 8 15 9 14 10 13 ....   7.____
   A. 12 11   B. 13 12   C. 11 13   D. 11 12   E. 11 14

8. 4 5 13 6 7 12 8 .0...   8.____
   A. 9 11   B. 13 9   C. 9 13   D. 11 9   E. 11 10

9. 3 8 4 9 5 10 6 11 7 ....   9.____
   A. 7 11   B. 7 8   C. 11 8   D. 12 7   E. 12 8

10. 18 14 19 17 20 20 21 ....   10.____
    A. 22 24   B. 14 19   C. 24 21   D. 21 23   E. 23 22

KEY (CORRECT ANSWERS)

1. B   6. E
2. D   7. D
3. E   8. A
4. A   1. E
5. E   2. E

EXAMINATION SECTION
TEST 1

DIRECTIONS: Each question or incomplete statement is followed by several suggested answers or completions. Select the one that BEST answers the question or completes the statement. *PRINT THE LETTER OF THE CORRECT ANSWER IN THE SPACE AT THE RIGHT.*

Questions 1-9.

DIRECTIONS: Questions 1 through 9 each consists of a series of numbers which follow in sequence according to a certain rule. Determine the rule and use it to select the next number from among the four choices given on the right side of each row.

SAMPLE X:

						(A)	(B)	(C)	(D)
3	6	9	12	15	18	19	20	21	22

In Sample X above, the rule is to add 3 to each successive number in the series in order to get the next number. Therefore, since 18 plus 3 is 21, the CORRECT choice is C.

SAMPLE Y:

						(A)	(B)	(C)	(D)
4	6	9	13	18	24	27	28	29	31

In Sample Y above, the rule is to add 2, then add 3, then add 4, etc., to each successive number in the series to get the next number. Therefore, the CORRECT choice is D.

1. 3   9   4   12   7   21
   A. 25
   B. 18
   C. 16
   D. 8

2. 5   3   6   3   9   5
   A. 20
   B. 18
   C. 10
   D. 3

3. 10   8   12   4   20   -12
   A. 52
   B. 48
   C. 0
   D. -26

4. 3   10   9   15   13   18
   A. 12
   B. 15
   C. 20
   D. 36

5. 1   1   3   9   13   65   A. 15   5.____
                                  B. 26
                                  C. 71
                                  D. 102

6. 2   6   5   15   13   39   A. 4   6.____
                                  B. 18
                                  C. 36
                                  D. 39

7. 48   8   40   10   30   15   A. 15   7.____
                                  B. 20
                                  C. 25
                                  D. 42

8. 20   5   30   10   50   25   A. 110   8.____
                                  B. 100
                                  C. 75
                                  D. 40

9. 4   24   12   60   20   80   A. 40   9.____
                                  B. 36
                                  C. 20
                                  D. 8

10. Below is a series of numbers. In this series, the numbers follow some definite order. Look   10.____
    at the numbers in the series and determine what the order is; then, from the suggested
    answers, consisting of two numbers each and lettered A, B, C, and D, choose the one
    that gives the next two numbers in the series.
    9 9 2 11 11 4 13

    A. 14 14   B. 13 6   C. 13 5   D. 14 6

11. In the letter series A, C, F, J, _____, the letter which logically belongs in the blank space   11.____
    is

    A. L   B. M   C. N   D. O

Questions 12-16.

DIRECTIONS: Each series of numbers is made up according to a certain rule or order. Indi-
              cate the NEXT number in the series.

12. 7, 21, 42, 126, 252, _____   12.____
    A. 275   B. 294   C. 378   D. 756

13. 4, 10, 7, 13, 10, 16, _____   13.____
    A. 13   B. 12   C. 14   D. 18

14. 9, 27, 25, 75, 73, 219, _____   14.____
    A. 217   B. 216   C. 222   D. 637

15. 3, 9, 10, 30, 31, 93, _____   15.____

    A. 91   B. 92   C. 94   D. 83

16. 12, 6, 24, 12, 48, 24, _____   16.____

    A. 72   B. 96
    C. 144   D. none of the above

Questions 17-20.

DIRECTIONS: Each question or incomplete statement is followed by several suggested answers or completions. Select the one that BEST answers the question or completes the statement.

17. The number which logically belongs in the blank box is   17.____

    | 6 | | 3 | | 9 |
    |---| |---| |---|
    | 12| | 18| | 7 |
    | 4 | | 1 | | |

    A. 6   B. 7   C. 8   D. 9

18. The number which logically belongs in the blank space is   18.____
    3, 5, 9, 17, _____

    A. 25   B. 33   C. 39   D. 41

19. The number which logically belongs in the blank box is   19.____

    | 3 | | 4 | | 2 |
    |---| |---| |---|
    | 6 | | 12| | |
    | 2 | | 3 | | 6 |

    A. 11   B. 12   C. 15   D. 16

20. The number which logically belongs in the blank space is   20.____

    4 → 10
    2 → 5
    3 → ?

    A. 11   B. 13   C. 16   D. 17

KEY (CORRECT ANSWERS)

1.	C	11.	D
2.	A	12.	D
3.	A	13.	A
4.	B	14.	A
5.	C	15.	C
6.	C	16.	B
7.	A	17.	A
8.	B	18.	B
9.	C	19.	B
10.	B	20.	D

TEST 2

DIRECTIONS: The following consists of a series of numbers which follow in sequence according to a certain rule. Determine the rule and use it to select the next number from among the four choices given on the right side of each row.

1. 16 13 10 7
    A. 3
    B. 5
    C. 19
    D. None of these

    1.____

2. 15 12 13 10 11 8 9
    A. 6
    B. 7
    C. 14
    D. None of these

    2.____

3. 33 36 31 34 29 32
    A. 28
    B. 30
    C. 35
    D. None of these

    3.____

4. 10 15 21 28 36
    A. 41
    B. 42
    C. 44
    D. None of these

    4.____

5. 9 7.2 5.4 3.6 1.8
    A. 0
    B. .8
    C. .9
    D. None of these

    5.____

6. 8 11 22 25 50 53 106
    A. 109
    B. 159
    C. 212
    D. None of these

    6.____

7. 8 1/3 7 5 2/3 4 1/3
    A. 2
    B. 2 2/3
    C. 3
    D. None of these

    7.____

8. 77 78 79 83 87 94 101
    A. 102
    B. 108
    C. 111
    D. None of these

    8.____

9. 40 42 47 44 46 51 48
    A. 46
    B. 50
    C. 53
    D. None of these

    9.____

17

2 (#2)

10. 21 24 32 36 44 49 57
  A. 60
  B. 63
  C. 65
  D. None of these
  10.____

11. 4 11 14 20 22 27
  A. 28
  B. 31
  C. 32
  D. None of these
  11.____

12. 2 1/6 3 1/3 4 1/2 5 2/3 6 5/6
  A. 7 1/2
  B. 8
  C. 9
  D. None of these
  12.____

13. 9 14 21 25 32 35 42
  A. 40
  B. 44
  C. 45
  D. None of these
  13.____

14. 99 91 87 78 73 63 57
  A. 46
  B. 49
  C. 68
  D. None of these
  14.____

15. 40 35 30 24 18 13
  A. 7
  B. 8
  C. 9
  D. None of these
  15.____

KEY (CORRECT ANSWERS)

1. D
2. A
3. D
4. D
5. A

6. A
7. C
8. C
9. B
10. B

11. A
12. B
13. B
14. A
15. B

TEST 3

DIRECTIONS: Each of the following series is made up according to some rule. Addition, subtraction, multiplication, division, or various combinations of these operations are used in forming each series. Discover the rule for each series and decide which of the four suggested answers is CORRECT as the next term. *PRINT THE LETTER OF THE CORRECT ANSWER IN THE SPACE AT THE RIGHT.*

Sample :   1   3   5   7
         A.   7   B. 8   C.   9   D.   10

The correct answer is C, since 9 is the next term in the series.

1. 12   0   10   0   8   0 _____   1.____
 A. 0   B. 6   C. 7   D. 10

2. 42   37   32   27 _____   2.____
 A. 22   B. 23   C. 24   D. 25

3. r^6 $6r$ r^5 $5r$ r^4 _____   3.____
 A. r^3 B. $3r$ C. $4r^3$ D. $4r$

4. 2   4   8   16   3   2 _____   4.____
 A. 46   B. 48   C. 54   D. 64

5. 8   11   14   17 _____   5.____
 A. 18   B. 19   C. 20   D. 21

6. 1   4   7   10   13 _____   6.____
 A. 17   B. 16   C. 15   D. 14

7. 4   5   7   8   10 _____   7.____
 A. 14   B. 13   C. 12   D. 11

8. 17   17   13   9   9 _____   8.____
 A. 4   B. 5   C. 6   D. 7

9. ab   4589   2ab   458   3ab _____   9.____
 A. 45   B. 58   C. 48   D. 4ab

10. $\dfrac{a+4}{2a}$ $\dfrac{a+10}{5a}$ $\dfrac{a+16}{8a}$ _____   10.____
 A. $\dfrac{a+18}{9a}$ B. $\dfrac{a+20}{11a}$ C. $\dfrac{a+22}{11a}$ D. $\dfrac{a+22}{12a}$

11. 64   32   16   8 _____
    A. 0   B. 2   C. 4   D. 6

12. 56342   xy²   5634   x2y³   563   x³y⁴ _____
    A. x^4y^5 B. y^4y^5 C. 63   D. 56

13. 48.08   24.04   12.02 _____
    A. 6.06   B. 6.02   C. 6.01   D. 6.1

14. 2   6   10   11   15   19 _____
    A. 20   B. 21   C. 22   D. 23

15. $2y^3$-10 $6y^8$-16 $10y^{13}$-22 _____
    A. $16y^{18}$-28   B. $16y^{16}$-24   C. $14y^{16}$-24   D. $14y^{18}$-28

16. $4y^8$ $5y^7$ $4y^6$ $7y^5$ $4y^4$ _____
    A. $5y^7$ B. $9y^3$ C. $4y^2$ D. $5y^3$

17. 2   5   9   14   20 _____
    A. 27   B. 26   C. 25   D. 24

18. 3   2   4   3   5   4 _____
    A. 6   B. 5   C. 4   D. 3

19. 2   4   6   7   9   11 _____
    A. 15   B. 14   C. 12   D. 11

20. 3   8   13   18   23 _____
    A. 31   B. 29   C. 28   D. 27

21. 1   3   6   10   15 _____
    A. 17   B. 19   C. 20   D. 21

22. 3/5   1 1/5   1 4/5   2 2/5 _____
    A. 2 1/2   B. 2 4/5   C. 3   D. 3 1/5

23. 2   4   8   14   22 _____
    A. 30   B. 32   C. 34   D. 36

24. 4   5   10   11   22   23 _____
    A. 24   B. 44   C. 45   D. 46

25. 1   3   7   15 _____
    A. 31   B. 29   C. 27   D. 22

2 (#3)

26. 24 23 22 20 19 18 _____   26.____
    A. 13   B. 14   C. 15   D. 16

27. 5/32 5/16 5/8 1 1/4 2 1/2 _____   27.____
    A. 5   B. 3 3/4   C. 3 1/2   D. 3 1/4

28. 5/108 5/36 5/12 5/4 3 3/4 _____   28.____
    A. 11 1/4   B. 7 1/4   C. 6 3/4   D. 6 1/4

29. 1 1 2 6 24 _____   29.____
    A. 124   B. 120   C. 96   D. 42

30. 1 4 9 16 _____   30.____
    A. 23   B. 24   C. 25   D. 27

KEY (CORRECT ANSWERS)

1.	B	16.	D
2.	A	17.	A
3.	D	18.	A
4.	D	19.	C
5.	D	20.	C
6.	B	21.	D
7.	D	22.	C
8.	B	23.	B
9.	A	24.	D
10.	C	25.	A
11.	C	26.	D
12.	D	27.	A
13.	C	28.	A
14.	A	29.	B
15.	D	30.	C

TEST 4

DIRECTIONS: Each question or incomplete statement is followed by several suggested answers or completions. Select the one that BEST answers the question or completes the statement. *PRINT THE LETTER OF THE CORRECT ANSWER IN THE SPACE AT THE RIGHT.*

1. 1, 2, 3, 4, _____
   A. 8   B. 7   C. 6   D. 5   1._____

2. 1, 5, 9, 13, _____
   A. 15   B. 17   C. 22   D. 19   2._____

3. A   B   D   E   G   H _____
   A. K   B. I   C. F   D. J   3._____

4. C, E, G, K, M, _____
   A. V   B. S   C. Q   D. R   4._____

5. A, D, G, J, _____
   A. L   B. M   C. N   D. K   5._____

6. b, c, d, f, g, h, _____
   A. i   B. j   C. k   D. l   6._____

7. f, e, d, c, _____
   A. 3, 4, 5, 6   B. 6, 5, 4, 3
   C. z, y, x. w   D. 2, 4, 6, 8   7._____

8. A, 1, D, 4, J, 10, M, _____
   A. 13   B. 14   C. 16   D. 18   8._____

9. 1, 3, 9, 27, _____
   A. 36   B. 69   C. 45   D. 81   9._____

10. 1203004000500 _____
    A. 600 B. 0   C. 006 D. 00   10._____

11. 1, 2, 4, 7, 11, _____
    A. 16   B. 14   C. 18   D. 15   11._____

12. 4, 9, 16, _____
    A. 23   B. 25   C. 27   D. 24   12._____

13. If A = B, then X = 101
    If A is greater than B, X = 102
    If A is less than B, X = 103
    If A = 0, X = 104.
    Now, if A - B = 3 and B is greater than O, then x =

    A. 101   B. 102   C. 103   D. 104

    13.____

14. 2000, 1999, 1996, 1991, _____

    A. 1986   B. 1899   C. 1984   D. 1987

    14.____

15. a = b, b ≠ c
    Which is NOT true?

    A. a + b ≠ c   B. a - 1 = c
    C. b + 1 = c   D. c - 1 = a

    15.____

16. 1, 8, 22, 50, _____

    A. 64   B. 106   C. 134   D. 100

    16.____

17. 3, 8, 15, 26, 39, _____

    A. 51   B. 45   C. 56   D. 47

    17.____

18. XooXXoXo _____

    A. oo   B. oX   C. Xo   D. XX

    18.____

19. XXoooo _____

    A. one o   B. 6 X's
    C. 5 X's   D. one o, three X's

    19.____

20. 4, 6, 8, 10, 14, _____

    A. 18   B. 20   C. 24   D. 16

    20.____

21. 2, 2, 4, 12, 48, _____

    A. 60   B. 96   C. 144   D. 240

    21.____

22. XoooXXXXX

    A. 3 X's, 2 o's   B. 5 o's
    C. 7 X's   D. 7 o's

    22.____

23. 2, 5, 13, 36, _____

    A. 72   B. 49   C. 68   D. 104

    23.____

24. XooXXXoo _____

    A. oX   B. Xo   C. XX   D. oo

    24.____

25. a   cd   ghi   mnop _____

    A. uvwx   B. vwxyz   C. wxyz   D. uvwxy

    25.____

KEY (CORRECT ANSWERS)

1.	D	11.	A
2.	B	12.	B
3.	D	13.	B
4.	C	14.	C
5.	B	15.	B
6.	B	16.	B
7.	B	17.	C
8.	A	18.	B
9.	D	19.	B
10.	C	20.	D

21. D
22. D
23. D
24. D
25. D

———

LETTER SERIES
CONTENTS

	Page
COMMENTARY	1
SAMPLE QUESTIONS	1
Sample Question 1	1
Explanation	1
Sample Question 2	2
Explanation	2
TEST 1	3
TEST 2	4
TEST 3	5
TEST 4	6
TEST 5	7
KEYS (CORRECT ANSWERS)	8

LETTER SERIES
COMMENTARY

Letter-series problems, also variously denoted as alphabetic series and/or progressions, constitute an important method for measuring quantitative ability on the part of senior and/or supervisory personnel as applicants for mid-level or senior-level positions.

Through this instrument, numerical reasoning—the usual technic for measuring mathematical ability—is substituted for by the comparatively abstract procedure of using letters instead of numbers—an admittedly more unusual and complex discipline.

Even more challenging than the number-series question, and of the highest order of difficulty, the letter-series question consists of a series of letters (instead of numbers) which is to be followed and carried forward (or backward) according to a definite order of sequence. Basically, the element of abstractness (i.e., letters instead of numbers) serves to compound this question.

A valuable, concrete suggestion to the examinee, as an aid in solving alphabetic-series problems, is to begin by writing out the alphabet (e.g., in columns of five letters) and keeping this visual aid immediately in front of him so that he may be enabled to solve the question more readily that way. Such a listing follows:

```
A   B   C   D   E
F   G   H   I   J
K   L   M   N   O
P   Q   R   S   T
U   V   W   X   Y
Z
```

SAMPLE QUESTIONS

DIRECTIONS: In each question in this test, there is, at the left, a series of several letters which follow some definite order, and, underneath, there are five sets of two letters each.
Look at the letters in the series at the left and find out what order they follow. Now decide what the next two letters in that series would be if the order were continued. Then find those two letters in one of the five sets of letters below and print the letter in the space at the right which has the same letter as the correct answer.

<u>SAMPLE QUESTION 1</u>
x c x d x e x
    A. f x   B. f g   C. x f   D. e f   E. x g

Explanation
    The order in this series is the letter *x* alternating with letters in a certain alphabetical order starting with *c* so that if the series were continued for two more letters, it would read
    x c x d x e x f x
and *f x* are those two letters lettered A, B, C, D, and E, in the above question, the set *f x* is labeled A. Therefore, you should indicate A on your answer sheet.

SAMPLE QUESTION
u u t t s s r
    A. r r   B. r q   C. q r   D. q q   E. r s

Explanation
    The order in this series is pairs of letters starting with *u u* and going backward through the alphabet so that if the series were continued for two more letters, it would read
    u u t t s s r r q
and *r q* are those two letters you would look for.
    In the five sets of letters lettered A, B, C, D, and E, in the above question, the set *r q* is labeled B. Therefore, you should indicate B on your answer sheet.

EXAMINATION SECTION
TEST 1

DIRECTIONS: In each series below determine what the order of the letters is and decide what the next two letters should be. From the suggested answers below, choose the one that gives the next two letters in the series. *PRINT THE LETTER OF THE CORRECT ANSWER IN THE SPACE AT THE RIGHT.*

1. x e x d x c x
   A. b x   B. a x   C. f x   D. g x   E. h x   1.____

2. r r s s t t u
   A. u u   B. u v   C. u s   D. v w   E. u w   2.____

3. a v a w a x a
   A. z a   B. y z   C. y a   D. a z   E. a y   3.____

4. a b d e g h j
   A. k l   B. l n   C. j m   D. l m   E. k m   4.____

5. a r c s e t g
   A. h i   B. h u   C. u j   D. u i   E. i v   5.____

6. m n o m n o m
   A. m n   B. n o   C. n m   D. o n   E. o m   6.____

7. e e a e e b e
   A. e e   B. e f   C. c e   D. f e   E. e c   7.____

8. f g g f h h f
   A. f f   B. f i   C. i i   D. i f   E. j j   8.____

9. p p q r r s t
   A. t t   B. u v   C. u u   D. t u   E. t v   9.____

10. l c d l e f l
    A. l g   B. g h   C. l e   D. f g   E. g g   10.____

TEST 2

DIRECTIONS: In each series below determine what the order of the letters is and decide what the next two letters should be. From the suggested answers below, choose the one that gives the next two letters in the series. *PRINT THE LETTER OF THE CORRECT ANSWER IN THE SPACE AT THE RIGHT.*

1. g n v h o w i
   A. p j   B. x j   C. i p   D. p x   E. x q

   1._____

2. r l s m t n u
   A. o v   B. u v   C. v w   D. o w   E. v o

   2._____

3. s h r i q j p
   A. k o   B. k l   C. o k   D. p k   E. o n

   3._____

4. a b z c d y e
   A. x g   B. x w   C. f w   D. f x   E. f g

   4._____

5. e e g i i k m
   A. m n   B. o o   C. o q   D. m o   E. n m

   5._____

6. j h n l r p v
   A. t x   B. s z   C. t z   D. s y   E. z t

   6._____

7. q g f i s k t
   A. u l   B. m u   C. l u   D. m n   E. l m

   7._____

8. e h i f i j g
   A. h i   B. j k   C. i k   D. j h   E. i j

   8._____

9. t g h e f v
   A. d c   B. d w   C. d e   D. c d   E. c w

   9._____

10. h g f k j i n
    A. m l   B. p o   C. l m   D. o p   E. m o

    10._____

TEST 3

DIRECTIONS: In each series below determine what the order of the letters is and decide what the next two letters should be. From the suggested answers below, choose the one that gives the next two letters in the series. *PRINT THE LETTER OF THE CORRECT ANSWER IN THE SPACE AT THE RIGHT.*

1. r p n l j h f
   A. e c   B. d c   C. e b   D. d b   E. e d
1._____

2. e g t h j t k
   A. l t   B. m t   C. l m   D. t l   E. m n
2._____

3. b d c e g f h
   A. g i   B. i k   C. j i   D. j l   E. j h
3._____

4. e h j m o r t
   A. v y   B. w z   C. v x   D. x z   E. w y
4._____

5. f r h t j v l
   A. m n   B. w y   C. x n   D. n w   E. x m
5._____

6. m p n q o r p
   A. s q   B. q r   C. t q   D. q s   E. s r
6._____

7. g i k h j l i
   A. k l   B. j k   C. j l   D. j m   E. k m
7._____

8. a c f h k m p
   A. s v   B. r t   C. r u   D. s u   E. q r
8._____

9. c d f g j k m
   A. n q   B. p q   C. o p   D. n p   E. o r
9._____

10. h g l m l q r
   A. q r   B. q w   C. r w   D. q v   E. r q
10._____

TEST 4

DIRECTIONS: In each series below determine what the order of the letters is and decide what the next two letters should be. From the suggested answers below, choose the one that gives the next two letters in the series. *PRINT THE LETTER OF THE CORRECT ANSWER IN THE SPACE AT THE RIGHT.*

1. c d f g j k o
   A. p t   B. p u   C. t x   D. t z   E. s x

   1.____

2. f d h f j h l
   A. j m   B. i n   C. j n   D. k m   E. i m

   2.____

3. r n p t p r v
   A. s u   B. r t   C. x z   D. z x   E. t r

   3.____

4. d f h h e g i i f h j
   A. j g   B. g g   C. g i   D. j i   E. l l

   4.____

5. y x v t s q o n l j i
   A. h f   B. h g   C. g e   D. f e   E. g f

   5.____

6. z x u q n l i
   A. f x   B. f b   C. d a   D. e b   E. g d

   6.____

7. c e i o c f k
   A. q c   B. r c   C. c p   D. r z   E. c q

   7.____

8. f g d i b k l
   A. i n   B. j h   C. a m   D. b e   E. c f

   8.____

9. m k h e k i f
   A. m g   B. h i   C. j d   D. c m   E. c i

   9.____

10. c e h l q o l
    A. q o   B. e c   C. n q   D. g d   E. h c

    10.____

TEST 5

DIRECTIONS: In each series below determine what the order of the letters is and decide what the next two letters should be. From the suggested answers below, choose the one that gives the next two letters in the series. *PRINT THE LETTER OF THE CORRECT ANSWER IN THE SPACE AT THE RIGHT.*

1. g i k h j l i
   A. h m   B. i k   C. l n   D. n m   E. k m

   1.____

2. z y z w y x y
   A. w w   B. w v   C. z y   D. v x   E. v w

   2.____

3. f g i j l m o
   A. q r   B. p q   C. p r   D. q s   E. r s

   3.____

4. b y x c d w v
   A. f e   B. w v   C. f u   D. e f   E. e v

   4.____

5. m l n k o j p
   A. i h   B. i q   C. q h   D. q m   E. o p

   5.____

6. y z x w u v t
   A. q r   B. q s   C. s r   D. r q   E. s q

   6.____

7. y v w t u r s
   A. p q   B. p o   C. q o   D. q r   E. w u

   7.____

8. h g s t f e u
   A. v c   B. v d   C. v w   D. w e   E. v e

   8.____

9. a k b j c i d
   A. e g   B. h e   C. e a   D. e h   E. g e

   9.____

10. a c d b e g h
    A. f i   B. e c   C. i k   D. j h   E. j l

    10.____

KEYS (CORRECT ANSWERS)

TEST 1	TEST 2	TEST 3	TEST 4	TEST 5
1. A	1. D	1. D	1. B	1. E
2. B	2. A	2. B	2. C	2. D
3. C	3. A	3. C	3. B	3. C
4. E	4. D	4. E	4. A	4. D
5. D	5. D	5. C	5. C	5. B
6. B	6. C	6. A	6. D	6. E
7. E	7. B	7. E	7. B	7. A
8. C	8. B	8. C	8. A	8. B
9. D	9. D	9. A	9. E	9. B
10. B	10. A	10. D	10. E	10. A

LETTER SERIES

COMMENTARY

Letter-series problems, also variously denoted as alphabetic series and/or progressions, constitute an important method for measuring quantitative ability on the part of senior and/or supervisory personnel as applicants for mid-level or senior-level positions.

Through this instrument, numerical reasoning - the usual technique for measuring mathematical ability - is substituted for by the comparatively abstract procedure of using letters instead of numbers -an admittedly more unusual and complex discipline.

Even more challenging than the number-series question, and of the highest order of difficulty, the letter-series question consists of a series of letters (instead of numbers), which is to be followed and carried forward (or backward) according to a definite order or sequence. Basically, the element of abstractness (i.e., letters instead of numbers) serves to compound this question.

A valuable, concrete suggestion to the examinee, as an aid in solving alphabetic-series problems, is to begin by writing out the alphabet (e.g., in columns of five letters) and keeping this visual aid immediately in front of him so that he may be enabled to solve the question more readily that way. Such a listing follows:

```
A    B    C    D    E
F    G    H    I    J
K    L    M    N    O
P    Q    R    S    T
U    V    W    X    Y
Z
```

SAMPLE QUESTIONS

DIRECTIONS: In each question in this test, there is, at the left, a series of several letters which follow some definite order, and, underneath, there are five sets of two letters each.

Look at the letters in the series at the left and find out what order they follow. Now decide what the next two letters in that series would be if the order were continued. Then find those two letters in one of the five sets of letters below and print in the space at the right the letter of the correct answer.

SAMPLE QUESTION 1   x c x d x e x
  A. f x   B. f g   C. x f   D. e f   E. x g

Explanation
The order in this series is the letter x alternating with letters in a certain alphabetical order starting with c so that if the series were continued for two or more letters, it would read:
                    x c x d x e x f x
and f x are those two letters you would look for.

In the five sets of letters lettered A, B, C, D, and E, in the above question, the set f x is labeled A. Therefore, you should indicate A in the space at the right.

SAMPLE QUESTION 2 u u t t s s r
A. r r   B. r q   C. q r   D. q q   E. r s

Explanation
The order in this series is pairs of letters starting with u u and going backward through the alphabet so that if the series were continued for two more letters, it would read:
u u t t s s r r q
and r q are those two letters you would look for.

In the five sets of letters lettered A, B, C, D, and E, in the above question, the set r q is labeled B. Therefore, you should indicate B in the space at the right.

EXAMINATION SECTION
TEST 1

DIRECTIONS: In each series below, determine what the order of the letters is and decide what the next two letters should be. From the suggested answers below, choose the one that gives the next two letters in the series and indicate the CORRECT answer in the space at the right. *PRINT THE LETTER OF THE CORRECT ANSWER IN THE SPACE AT THE RIGHT.*

1. A Z B Y C
   A. D W B. W D C. X D D. D X
   1.____

2. A C F J
   A. O U B. O W C. N U D. N W
   2.____

3. Z X V T
   A. S Q B. S R C. R Q D. R P
   3.____

4. M N O L K P Q
   A. J I B. S T C. J S D. I T
   4.____

5. Y Z A B W X C
   A. V D B. D U C. U D D. D V
   5.____

6. A B B C D D E F F
   A. G G B. G H C. H H D. H I
   6.____

7. Q A B Q B C Q C D
   A. E Q B. D Q C. Q E D. Q D
   7.____

8. L A M Z L B M Y L
   A. C X B. C M C. M C D. M X
   8.____

9. Y Z A W X B U
   A. V C B. C D C. C X D. V D
   9.____

10. N M Z M N Y N M X
    A. N M B. N W C. M N D. M W
    10.____

11. A Z W T B Q N K C
    A. I F B. I E C. H E D. H F
    11.____

12. Z Y Y X X X W W W W
    A. W V B. V V C. V U D. U U
    12.____

13. A D F I K
    A. N Q B. N P C. M Q D. M P
    13.____

37

2 (#1)

14. Z V S O L H   14.____
    A. E A   B. C E   C. E C   D. E B

15. A A B B B B A A A B B B B B A A A A   15.____
    A. A A   B. A B   C. B A   D. B B

16. W T U R S P   16.____
    A. Q N   B. M N   C. O R   D. R N

17. E I G K I M K   17.____
    A. O K   B. N K   C. O M   D. N M

18. H A B C H B C D H   18.____
    A. C D   B. D E   C. A C   D. C E

19. A C E E G I K K M   19.____
    A. Q Q   B. O O   C. O Q   D. N Q

20. Z Y X X X W V U U U T   20.____
    A. T S   B. S S   C. T R   D. S R

KEY (CORRECT ANSWERS)

1.	C	11.	C
2.	A	12.	B
3.	D	13.	B
4.	A	14.	A
5.	B	15.	D
6.	B	16.	A
7.	D	17.	C
8.	B	18.	A
9.	A	19.	C
10.	C	20.	D

TEST 2

DIRECTIONS: In each series below, determine what the order of the letters is and decide what the next letters should be. From the suggested answers below, choose the one that gives the letters in the series and indicate the CORRECT answer in the space at the right. *PRINT THE LETTER OF THE CORRECT ANSWER IN THE SPACE AT THE RIGHT.*

1. A B C C C D E F F F G H   1.____
   A. H H   B. H I   C. I J   D. I I

2. Z X X V T R R   2.____
   A. R P   B. P P   C. P M   D. P N

3. L A B B L B C C L   3.____
   A. D D   B. C D   C. D E   D. C E

4. Y U W W Y U T T Y   4.____
   A. U Q   B. Y U   C. Q Q   D. U U

5. B E D C F E D   5.____
   A. E G   B. G F   C. F G   D. G H

6. Z Z Y Y Y X X W W W V   6.____
   A. V V   B. U U   C. V U   D. U T

7. A D F I K N   7.____
   A. R T   B. P R   C. P S   D. Q S

8. W U T R Q   8.____
   A. P O   B. P N   C. O N   D. O M

9. B C C E F F   9.____
   A. H I   B. G H   C. H J   D. G G

10. A Z Y B C X   10.____
    A. W D   B. D V   C. D W   D. W V

11. P K A P K C P   11.____
    A. K D   B. K E   C. P E   D. D K

12. A B C Z A B C Y A   12.____
    A. C X   B. B X   C. B C   D. C B

13. L A B B C L B C C D   13.____
    A. D L   B. L C   C. L E   D. L D

2 (#2)

14. M M A Z M M A Y M M   14. ____
    A. MA   B. AB   C. MX   D. AX

15. Z Z Z Y X X X W V   15. ____
    A. VV   B. VU   C. UU   D. UV

16. M N O P N O P M O P M N   16. ____
    A. PM   B. OP   C. MO   D. PN

17. G H I I H I G G I G   17. ____
    A. HI   B. IH   C. HH   D. HG

18. A E F B F E C E F   18. ____
    A. GF   B. DE   C. GE   D. DF

19. J A J J B J J J C   19. ____
    A. JJ   B. JD   C. JE   D. DJ

20. E H G J I L   20. ____
    A. ON   B. KN   C. KM   D. OM

KEY (CORRECT ANSWERS)

1.	D	11.	B
2.	D	12.	C
3.	B	13.	B
4.	A	14.	D
5.	B	15.	A
6.	C	16.	A
7.	C	17.	C
8.	C	18.	D
9.	A	19.	A
10.	A	20.	B

TEST 3

DIRECTIONS: In each series below, determine what the order of the letters is and decide what the next letters should be. From the suggested answers below, choose the one that gives the letters in the series and indicate the CORRECT answer in the space at the right. *PRINT THE LETTER OF THE CORRECT ANSWER IN THE SPACE AT THE RIGHT.*

1. A B B A C C A D D   1._____
   A. E E A   B. A A E   C. A E E   D. E E E

2. A C E G I   2._____
   A. J K L   B. K N P   C. K M O   D. J L N

3. Z Z Y X X W V   3._____
   A. V U U   B. U U T   C. U T T   D. V U T

4. Z X Y W U V T   4._____
   A. R Q P   B. R S Q   C. S Q R   D. R P Q

5. C B B A D C C B E   5._____
   A. D C C   B. D D C   C. E D D   D. E D C

6. X Y Z Z V W X X T U   6._____
   A. V V R   B. U V S   C. U V R   D. V V S

7. M N L O K P J   7._____
   A. Q I R   B. I Q R   C. Q R I   D. I R Q

8. M Y Z K W X I   8._____
   A. J U V   B. J V U   C. U V G   D. U V H

9. D A B C H E F G   9._____
   A. H L K   B. L I J   C. L J K   D. H K J

10. A A D D D G G J J J   10._____
    A. M M O   B. M P P   C. M N N   D. M M P

11. L N N L L N N N L L L   11._____
    A. N N L   B. N L L   C. L L L   D. N N N

12. F G H H G H F F H   12._____
    A. H F G   B. F F G   C. H F F   D. F G G

13. Z A B Y X C D   13._____
    A. W U E   B. W V E   C. E W V   D. E V U

14. AMNBMMNCMMMN

    A. DMM   B. DMN   C. DNN   D. DNM

15. YOYOPYOPQY

    A. ORY   B. OPQ   C. PQY   D. OQR

16. DCABHGEFL

    A. KIJ   B. KJI   C. IJK   D. IKJ

17. AMNENMIMN

    A. MMN   B. NMN   C. NNM   D. MNM

18. TZXVTTZXVVTTT

    A. ZZX   B. ZXV   C. XZZ   D. XVZ

19. ABZBAYABXB

    A. WAB   B. AWB   C. AWA   D. WBA

20. RASACRACESA

    A. CGR   B. COS   C. CEG   D. CER

KEY (CORRECT ANSWERS)

1. C		11. D	
2. C		12. D	
3. D		13. B	
4. B		14. A	
5. B		15. B	
6. A		16. A	
7. A		17. D	
8. C		18. B	
9. B		19. C	
10. D		20. C	

TEST 4

DIRECTIONS: In each series below, determine what the order of the letters is and decide what the next two letters should be. From the suggested answers below, choose the one that gives the next two letters in the series and indicate the CORRECT answer in the space at the right. *PRINT THE LETTER OF THE CORRECT ANSWER IN THE SPACE AT THE RIGHT.*

1. DZDZYDZYXDZ 1.____
   A. YXW   B. YDX   C. YXD   D. DYW

2. YZAWXBUVC 2.____
   A. DST   B. SDE   C. DES   D. STD

3. FALGALLHALLL 3.____
   A. ILL   B. IAL   C. LIL   D. LAI

4. AMNOCONMEMNOG 4.____
   A. OMN   B. MON   C. MNO   D. ONM

5. DCBAHGFELK 5.____
   A. IJL   B. JIP   C. JIO   D. IJM

6. WXYZXYZWYZXWZ 6.____
   A. YXW   B. YWX   C. WXY   D. WYX

7. BJKLBBJKLLBBBJ 7.____
   A. KLL   B. KKL   C. LKB   D. LLB

8. RSCBASRABCRSC 8.____
   A. BAS   B. ABS   C. ASB   D. BSA

9. VVVTVVTTVTTT 9.____
   A. VVV   B. TTT   C. TTV   D. VVT

10. AZXDVTGRP 10.____
    A. KNM   B. JOM   C. JNL   D. KON

11. AEIBFJCGKD 11.____
    A. IME   B. ILE   C. HME   D. HLE

12. CCMNOPCCNOPQCCOPQR 12.____
    A. CCQ   B. CCP   C. CPQ   D. CQR

13. LOMNJQKPH 13.____
    A. SRI   B. RIS   C. SIR   D. RSI

2 (#4)

14. Y Y Y B B W W W D D U U   14.____
    A. F F S   B. U F F   C. F F F   D. U F S

15. P Q R Z Z Q R P Y Y R P Q X X P   15.____
    A. Q W W   B. Q R W   C. R Q W   D. R R W

16. K D E K D F K D G K   16.____
    A. D H K   B. H D K   C. D I K   D. I K D

17. M L A K J B I H C   17.____
    A. G F E   B. D E F   C. D F G   D. G F D

18. Z K Z Z L Z K Z Z M Z K Z Z   18.____
    A. K N Z   B. N Z Z   C. K Z N   D. N Z K

19. A R R B R C R R D R E   19.____
    A. R F R   B. F R R   C. R R F   D. F F R

20. C B A X F E D X I H G X   20.____
    A. J K L   B. L J X   C. L K J   D. J K X

KEY (CORRECT ANSWERS)

1.	A	11.	D
2.	D	12.	B
3.	B	13.	C
4.	D	14.	B
5.	B	15.	B
6.	C	16.	A
7.	A	17.	D
8.	A	18.	D
9.	B	19.	C
10.	C	20.	C

TEST 5

DIRECTIONS: In each of the following questions, there is a series of letters and numbers which follow some definite order, and underneath there are four sets of two or three letters each. Look at the letters and numbers in the series and determine what the order is. Then, from the suggested answers below, select the set that gives the next set of letters in the series in their correct order. *PRINT THE LETTER OF THE CORRECT ANSWER N THE SPACE AT THE RIGHT.*

1. A Z 1 Y B 2 C X
   A. D 3   B. 3 D   C. 3 W   D. W 3

2. Y 2 W 3 U 2 S 3
   A. Q 3   B. R 3   C. Q 2   D. R 2

3. Y Z A 9 W X B 8 U V
   A. 7 D   B. C D   C. W 7   D. C 7

4. I I Q A B 2 1 Q B C 3 1 Q C D 4
   A. 1 D E   B. 5 Q E   C. 5 Q 1   D. 1 Q D

5. N M 8 Z M N 5 Y N M 8 X
   A. M N 5   B. N M 5   C. M N 8   D. N M 8

6. A 1 D 9 G 2 J 8
   A. M 7   B. N 3   C. M 3   D. N 7

7. A A 8 9 B B 9 8 C C 8
   A. 8 D   B. 9 D   C. 9 E   D. 8 E

8. 4 4 H A B C 5 4 H D E F 6 4 H G
   A. H I 4   B. I 7 4   C. H 7 4   D. H I 7

9. Z 7 X X Y 7 7 X X X 7 7 7 X X
   A. W 7   B. 7 7   C. 7 W   D. W X

10. B D 1 2 B F 2 3 B H 3 4 B
    A. I 5 6   B. J 5 6   C. I 4 5   D. J 4 5

11. Y W 1 1 2 U S 1 1 3 Q 0 1 1 4
    A. M L S   B. N M 5   C. M K 1   D. N L 1

12. A C 6 B D 5 C E 6
    A. D F   B. D 5   C. F 5   D. F G

13. 2 P K A 2 P K B 2 P
    A. K 2   B. P K   C. P C   D. K C

45

2 (#5)

14. MM33AMM44BM 14.____
    A. M5C   B. M55   C. 55C   D. 5CM

15. LALL9LAMM8LA 15.____
    A. N7L   B. NN7   C. NNL   D. NL7

16. ACD4EGH5I 16.____
    A. KL6   B. JL6   C. JK6   D. KM6

17. C1BBAF2EEDI3H 17.____
    A. GG4   B. HGL   C. G4L   D. HG4

18. 42MN24L042KP2 18.____
    A. 2JR   B. 4JQ   C. 4QJ   D. JQ2

19. 3Y3YA3YAB3YABC3 19.____
    A. YCD   B. YAD   C. YAB   D. YBC

20. 543DZ543DY54 20.____
    A. 3DX   B. 3EX   C. 3DE   D. 3ED

KEY (CORRECT ANSWERS)

1.	C	11.	C
2.	C	12.	A
3.	D	13.	D
4.	D	14.	B
5.	A	15.	B
6.	C	16.	A
7.	B	17.	B
8.	D	18.	B
9.	A	19.	C
10.	D	20.	A

NUMBER AND LETTER SERIES

COMMENTARY

One of the most searching types of the arithmetic reasoning question—a basic staple of tests of general and mental ability—is the number-series problem, in which a series of single numbers (or paired numbers) is presented, which follow a certain rule or sequence. The examinee is to select the next number (or pair of numbers) if the series were to be continued in this manner.

More difficult still, and on the highest level of difficulty is the letter-series question, wherein a series of letters, instead of numbers, is to be followed according to a definite order. Here, the element of abstractness serves to add further complexity to the problem.

Suggestion: In solving alphabetic series and progressions, it is wise to write out the alphabet and keep it in front of you. With this visual and aid immediately available, the key to each series can then be solved much more easily that way.

The questions in this section test your ability to see relationships between the elements of a series. These questions are sometimes referred to as series or progressions, and, in them, the candidate is asked to determine the rule that binds the elements together and then select the following element(s) according to that rule.

NUMBER SERIES/ONE NUMBER

SAMPLE QUESTIONS

DIRECTIONS: Each of the three sample questions presents a series of six numbers. Each series of numbers is made up according to a certain rule or order. You are to find what the next number in the series should be if the series were to be continued in this sequence.

1. 2 4 6 8 10 12
    A. 14   B. 16   C. 18
    D. 20   E. None of the above

Explanation: In Question 1, the rule is to add 2 to each number (2+2 = 4; 4 + 2 = 6, etc.). The net number in the series is 14 (12+2 = 14). Since 14 is lettered A among the suggested answers, A is the correct answer.

2. 7 8 6 7 5 6
    A. 2   B. 3   C. 4
    D. 5   E. None of the above

Explanation: In Question 2, the rule is to add 1 to the first number, subtract 2 from the next, add 1, subtract 2, and so on. The next number in the series is 4; letter C is the correct answer.

3. 3 6 9 12 15 18

Explanation: In Question 3, the rule is to add 3, making 21 the next number in the series. The correct answer to Question 3 is *none of the above*, since 39, 40, 45, and 59 are all incorrect answers; therefore, E is the correct answer.

NUMBER SERIES/ONE NUMBER

EXAMINATION SECTION

TEST 1

DIRECTIONS: Each of the following questions presents a series of single numbers. Five possible answers are given. From these choices, you are to find what the next number in the series should be if the series were to be continued in this sequence. *PRINT THE LETTER OF THE CORRECT ANSWER IN THE SPACE AT THE RIGHT.*

1. 3 13 4 15 5 7 6 19 7
   A. 20   B. 23   C. 21   D. 25   D. 27   1.____

2. 20 25 23 28 26 31 29 34
   A. 33   B. 32   C. 31   D. 30   E. 34   2.____

3. 9 24 39 54 69 84 99 114
   A. 129   B. 124   C. 128   D. 130   E. 126   3.____

4. 20 29 37 44 50 55 59
   A. 61   B. 62   C. 63   D. 64   E. 66   4.____

5. 20 21 23 26 30 35 41 48
   A. 55   B. 56   C. 54   D. 59   E. 57   5.____

6. 8 10 14 20 28 38 50 64
   A. 80   B. 72   C. 71   D. 73   E. 75   6.____

7. 6 7 9 12 16 21 28 35
   A. 40   B. 47   C. 50   D. 45   E. 43   7.____

8. 8 11 16 24 34 47
   A. 61   B. 62   C. 55   D. 60   E. 63   8.____

9. 3 8 14 25 37 54
   A. 67   B. 69   C. 68   D. 70   E. 72   9.____

10. 5 15 23 29 39 47 53 63
    A. 71   B. 72   C. 69   D. 73   E. 70   10.____

KEY (CORRECT ANSWERS)

1.	C	6.	A
2.	B	7.	E
3.	A	8.	B
4.	B	9.	E
5.	B	10.	A

TEST 2

DIRECTIONS: Each of the following questions presents a series of single numbers. Five possible answers are given. From these choices, you are to find what the next number in the series should be if the series were to be continued in this sequence. *PRINT THE LETTER OF THE CORRECT ANSWER IN THE SPACE AT THE RIGHT.*

1. 2 4 8 16 32 64 128
   A. 228   B. 130   C. 248   D. 264   E. 256

   1.____

2. 4 8 16 24 32 40 48
   A. 64   B. 56   C. 96   D. 62   E. 84

   2.____

3. 2 4 4 8 8 16 16
   A. 54   B. 48   C. 16   D. 32   E. 36

   3.____

4. 3 6 18 36 108 216 648
   A. 1946   B. 1944   C. 1296   D. 1056   E. 1488

   4.____

5. 10 13 11 14 12 15 13
   A. 14   B. 11   C. 15   D. 17   E. 16

   5.____

6. 2 6 18 54 162 486
   A. 1556   B. 496   C. 1286   D. 1458   E. 1552

   6.____

7. 4 20 35 49 62 74
   A. 82   B. 85   C. 93   D. 94   E. 96

   7.____

8. 10 15 12 17 14 19
   A. 22   B. 24   C. 21   D. 14   E. 16

   8.____

9. 4 10 8 14 12 18
   A. 16   B. 20   C. 24   D. 22   E. 21

   9.____

10. 10 18 15 23 20 28
    A. 23   B. 24   C. 25   D. 36   E. 40

    10.____

KEY (CORRECT ANSWERS)

1.	E	6.	D
2.	B	7.	B
3.	D	8.	E
4.	C	9.	A
5.	E	10.	C

TEST 3

NUMBER SERIES/TWO NUMBERS

SAMPLE QUESTIONS

DIRECTIONS: These questions are more difficult. In these, the arrangement is more complicated, and the answer is chosen from groups of two numbers, of which one group gives the next two numbers in the series

1. 1 1 2 1 3 1 4   1.____
   A. 1 5   B. 4 1   C. 5 1   D. 5 5   E. 6 1

Explanation: The series consists of 1's alternating with numbers in ascending numerical order. The next two numbers would be 5 and 1. Therefore, C is the correct answer.

2. 2 8 3 7 5 6 8 5   2.____
   A. 10 6   B. 11 3   C. 11 4   D. 12 4   E. 12 6

Explanation: This series consists of a sub-series for which the rule is to add 1, add 2, add 3, and add 4, alternating with another series in descending numerical order. The next number in the first sub-series would be 8 + 4, or 12; and the next number in the descending series would be 4. Therefore, D is the correct answer.

DIRECTIONS: Each of the following questions presents a series of single numbers. Five possible answers are given. From these choices, you are to find what the next number in the series should be if the series were to be continued in this sequence. *PRINT THE LETTER OF THE CORRECT ANSWER IN THE SPACE AT THE RIGHT.*

1. 3 4 3 5 3 6 3 7 3   1.____
   A. 8 3   B. 9 3   C. 9 4   D. 4 8   E. 7 5

2. 50 2 48 4 6 6 44   2.____
   A. 8 4 6   B. 8 4 2   C. 4 2 8   D. 4 4 8   E. 8 4 4

3. 40 39 43 38 6 37 49 36   3.____
   A. 3 7 5 1   B. 3 9 5 2   C. 5 1 3 7   D. 3 5 5 2   E. 5 2 3 5

4. 50 51 49 53 47 56 44 60 40   4.____
   A. 60 40   B. 35 60   C. 60 35   D. 65 35   E. 35 65

5. 1 100 2 50 4 25 8   5.____
   A. 12.5 4   B. 12.5 16   C. 16 12.5   D. 8.25 16   E. 16 8.25

6. 1 25 2 24 4 22 7 19 11   6.____
   A. 15 16   B. 16 16   C. 16 15   D. 18 17   E. 17 18

7. 2 4 6 8 12 14 18 20   7.____
   A. 26 22   B. 26 24   C. 22 26   D. 21 24   E. 24 26

51

2 (#3)

8. 1 2 4 8 16 32
   A. 48 64   B. 64 128   C. 64 72   D. 63 129   E. 72 64

8.____

9. 10 50 13 54 16 58 19 62
   A. 22 66   B. 66 22   C. 64 20   D. 66 20   E. 20 66

9.____

10. 2 60 12 58 22 56 32
   A. 36 46   B. 42 54   C. 56 42   D. 42 56   E. 54 42

10.____

11. 2 90 4 80 6 70 8 60
   A. 12 52   B. 50 10   C. 10 50   D. 12 50   E. 50 12

11.____

12. 10 70 11 67 13 64 16 61
   A. 19 58   B. 20 58   C. 18 58   D. 58 20   E. 58 19

12.____

13. 10 20 30 12 23 26 14 26 22 16
   A. 19 29   B. 29 18   C. 29 19   D. 18 29   E. 30 18

13.____

14. 2 5 4 6 8 8 14 11 22 15
   A. 32 20   B. 30 20   C. 20 32   D. 31 21   E. 20 30

14.____

15. 10 15 20 11 17 23 12 19 26 13 21 29 14
   A. 16 29   B. 15 23   C. 23 32   D. 32 23   E. 23 15

15.____

KEY (CORRECT ANSWERS)

1.	A	6.	A	11.	C
2.	B	7.	E	12.	B
3.	E	8.	B	13.	B
4.	D	9.	A	14.	A
5.	B	10.	E	15.	C

TEST 4

DIRECTIONS: Each of the following questions presents a series of single numbers. Five possible answers are given. From these choices, you are to find what the next number in the series should be if the series were to be continued in this sequence. *PRINT THE LETTER OF THE CORRECT ANSWER IN THE SPACE AT THE RIGHT.*

1. 150 120 149 118 147 114 044 108 140   1.____
   A. 104 138   B. 102 136   C. 135 140   D. 100 135   E. 135 100

2. 10 11 12 11 12 13 12 13 14 13 14 15 14   2.____
   A. 15 16   B. 13 14   C. 14 15   D. 16 15   E. 15 14

3. 2 4 5 6 11 10 20 16 32 24   3.____
   A. 34 46   B. 32 46   C. 48 32   D. 46 32   E. 47 34

4. 1 2 3 2 4 6 3 6 9 4 8 12 5   4.____
   A. 9 15   B. 9 14   C. 11 16   D. 10 14   E. 10 15

5. 1 2 3 4 4 4 7 6 5 10 8 6   5.____
   A. 10 13   B. 13 10   C. 12 10   D. 12 9   E. 10 9

6. 1 2 3 5 5 7 9 8 11 13 11   6.____
   A. 15 17   B. 17 15   C. 18 15   D. 15 18   E. 16 18

7. 10 12 13 14 15 17 18 19 20 22   7.____
   A. 23 24   B. 24 23   C. 23 23   D. 22 24   E. 24 22

8. 2 3 4 4 8 6 10 7 14 9 16 10 20 12   8.____
   A. 13 22   B. 12 24   C. 20 12   D. 24 12   E. 22 13

9. 1 2 2 5 4 9 5 12 7 16 8 19 10 23   9.____
   A. 27 12   B. 12 27   C. 11 26   D. 26 11   E. 12 28

10. 100 106 98 103 97 99 95 96 94 92 92 89 91 85   10.____
    A. 82 89   B. 89 82   C. 90 81   D. 81 90   E. 90 83

KEY (CORRECT ANSWERS)

1.	D	6.	A
2.	A	7.	A
3.	E	8.	E
4.	E	9.	C
5.	B	10.	B

TEST 5

LETTER SERIES

SAMPLE QUESTIONS

DIRECTIONS: In each of these questions, there is a series of letters which follow some definite order, and underneath there are five sets of two letters each. Look at the letters in the series and determine what the order is; then, from the suggested answers below, select the set that gives the next two letters in the series in their correct order.

1. X C X D X E X
   A. F X   B. F G   C. X F   D. E F   E. X G   1.____

Explanation: The series consists of X's alternating with letters in alphabetical order. The next two letters would be F and X; therefore, A is the correct answer.

2. A B D C E F H
   A. G H   B. I G   C. G I   D. K L   E. I H   2.____

Explanation: If you compare this series with the alphabet, you will find that it goes along in pairs, the first pair in their usual order and the next pair in reverse order. The last letter given in the series is the second letter of the pair G-H, which is in reverse order. The first missing letter must, therefore, be G. The next pair of letters would be I-J, in that order; the second of the missing letters is I. The alternative you look for, then, is G I, which is lettered C.

DIRECTIONS: Each of the following questions presents a series of single letters. Five possible answers are given. From these choices, find what the next letter in the series should be if the series were to continue in this sequence. *PRINT THE LETTER OF THE CORRECT ANSWER IN THE SPACE AT THE RIGHT.*

1. B A C A D A E A F A G A
   A. H A   B. A H   C. K A   D. L A   E. A K   1.____

2. A B D C B D D B D E B D F B D G B
   A. H D   B. B G   C. D B   D. D H   E. D J   2.____

3. J I H G F E D C
   A. BC   B. CB   C. BA   D. A B   E. DC   3.____

4. Z Y X W V U T S R
   A. PQ   B. P O   C. OP   D. N P   E. Q P   4.____

5. X W V X U X T X S X R
   A. X O   B. Q X   C. X P   D. P X   E. X Q   5.____

6. K L N M O P R Q S T
   A. V U   B. U V   C. W V   D. V W   E. W U   6.____

7. A B C F E D G H I L K J M
   A. O N   B. N O   C. O M   D. M O   E. M N   7.____

2 (#5)

8. Z Y W X V U S T R Q O P N M
   A. K J   B. J K   C. K L   D. L K   E. L M

   8.____

9. Y Z X W U V T S Q R P O M N
   A. K J   B. L K   C. K L   D. J K   E. M L

   9.____

10. Z Y X U V W T S R O P Q N M L
    A. I K   B. K I   C. I J   D. K J   E. J I

    10.____

11. A C E G I K M O Q
    A. S U   B. S T   C. R S   D. R T   E. U S

    11.____

12. Z U X V T R P N L
    A. K L   B. K J   C. H J   D. L K   E. J H

    12.____

13. Z W T Q N K H
    A. E B   B. E C   D. F B   D. F C   E. C F

    13.____

14. A D G J M P S
    A. V W   B. U W   C. U V   D. V Y   E. W U

    14.____

15. A D F I K N P S
    A. W U   B. U W   C. U X   D. U V   E. V U

    15.____

KEY (CORRECT ANSWERS)

1.	A	6.	A	11.	A
2.	D	7.	B	12.	E
3.	C	8.	C	13.	A
4.	E	9.	B	14.	D
5.	E	10.	E	15.	C

TEST 6

DIRECTIONS: Each of the following questions presents a series of single letters. Five possible answers are given. From these choices, you are to find what the next letter in the series should be if the series were to be continued in this sequence. *PRINT THE LETTER OF THE CORRECT ANSWER IN THE SPACE AT THE RIGHT.*

1. A C E D G I H K M L   1.____
    A. O P   B. O Q   C. Q P   D. P Q   E. Q O

2. Z X V W T R S P N O   2.____
    A. J K   B. K J   C. L K   D. K L   E. K I

3. B A D C F E H G J I L   3.____
    A. K N   B. K M   C. N K   D. L K   E. K L

4. Y Z W X U V S T Q R O P M   4.____
    A. L K   B. K L   C. N L   D. N K   E. L N

5. A B D C E F H G I J L K M N   5.____
    A. R P   B. P O   C. O P   D. P Q   E. Q P

6. A B C D F E G H I J L K M   6.____
    A. O N   B. N O   C. P O   D. O P   E. M N

7. Z Y X U V W T S R   7.____
    A. O P   B. P O   C. O N   D. N O   E. P Q

8. A B C B C D C D E D E F E   8.____
    A. G H   B. G F   C. E F   D. F G   E. F E

9. X V T R P F H J   9.____
    A. K L   B. L M   C. K M   D. M N   E. L N

10. C C F F I I L L V V S S P P M M   10.____
    A. K K   B. I I   C. J J   D. H H   E. G G

11. A N C O E P G   11.____
    A. H I   B. R H   C. R I   D. Q I   E. I Q

12. B D F H J L N   12.____
    A. P Q   B. S Q   C. R P   D. P R   E. Q S

13. Z X V T R P N   13.____
    A. J L   B. M L   C. L K   D. M K   E. L J

14. A B D G K   14.____
    A. L O   B. O Q   C. Q O   D. P L   E. P W

15. F H K O T R O
    A. J G   B. L F   C. K G   D. J F   E. K F   15._____

KEY (CORRECT ANSWERS)

1.	B	6.	B	11.	D
2.	E	7.	A	12.	D
3.	A	8.	D	13.	E
4.	D	9.	E	14.	E
5.	B	10.	C	15.	E

TEST 7

DIRECTIONS: Each of the following questions presents a series of single letters. Five possible answers are given. From these choices, you are to find what the next letter in the series should be if the series were to be continued in this sequence. *PRINT THE LETTER OF THE CORRECT ANSWER IN THE SPACE AT THE RIGHT.*

1. B B G G L L O O R R S S
   A. U U   B. V V   C. T T   D. W W   E. X X

   1.____

2. A C B D C E D F E G
   A. F G   B. G H   C. H F   D. F H   E. G F

   2.____

3. D H F J H L J N
   A. M N   B. L N   C. L O   D. L P   E. P N

   3.____

4. A C E F H J K M O
   A. M O Q   B. R T P   C. N Q O   D. P T R   E. P R T

   4.____

5. B G L Q V E J O
   A. P U   B. T Y   C. R W   D. S X   E. Y Z

   5.____

6. A F G B G H C H I D
   A. F K   B. G L   C. H M   D. I N   E. I J

   6.____

7. A K B L C M D N
   A. E M   B. F N   C. J L   D. E J   E. E O

   7.____

8. P R K M F H
   A. C E   B. A C   C. D F   D. B D   E. C E

   8.____

9. A G M S Y B H N
   A. P V   B. Q W   C. R X   D. S Y   E. T Z

   9.____

10. B E C F D G Y V X U
    A. W T   B. W V   C. V U   D. T S   E. U T

    10.____

KEY (CORRECT ANSWERS)

1.	C	6.	E
2.	D	7.	E
3.	D	8.	B
4.	E	9.	E
5.	B	10.	A

ABSTRACT REASONING

COMMENTARY

Since intelligence exists in many forms or phases and the theory of differential aptitudes is now firmly established in testing, other manifestations and measurements of intelligence than verbal or purely arithmetical must be identified and measured.

Classification inventory, or figure classification, involves the aptitude of form perception, i.e., the ability to perceive pertinent detail in objects or in pictorial or graphic material. It involves making visual comparisons and discriminations and discerning slight differences in shapes and shading figures and widths and lengths of lines.

Leading examples of presentation are the figure analogy and the figure classification. The section that follows presents progressive and varied samplings of this type of question.

SAMPLE QUESTIONS

DIRECTIONS: In each of these sample questions, look at the symbols in the first two boxes. Something about the three symbols in the first box makes them alike; something about the two symbols in the other box with the question mark makes them alike. Look for some characteristic that is common to all symbols in the same box, yet makes them different from the symbols in the other box. Among the five answer choices, find the symbol that can BEST be substituted for the question mark, because it is *like* the symbols in the second box, and, for the same reason, different from those in the first box.

1.

In sample question 1, all the symbols in the first box are vertical lines. The second box has two lines, one broken and one solid. Their *likeness* to each other consists in their being horizontal; and their being horizontal makes them *different* from the vertical lines in the other box. The answer must be the only one of the five lettered choices that is a horizontal line, ether broken or solid. Therefore, the CORRECT answer is C.

2.

The CORRECT answer is A.

EXAMINATION SECTION

TEST 1

DIRECTIONS: In each of these questions, look at the symbols in the first two boxes. Something about the three symbols in the first box makes them alike; something about the two symbols in the other box with the question mark makes them alike. Look for some characteristic that is common to all symbols in the same box, yet makes them different from the symbols in the other box. Among the five answer choices, find the symbol that can BEST be substituted for the question mark, because it is *like* the symbols in the second box, and, for the same reason, different from those in the first box. *PRINT THE LETTER OF THE CORRECT ANSWER IN THE SPACE AT THE RIGHT.*

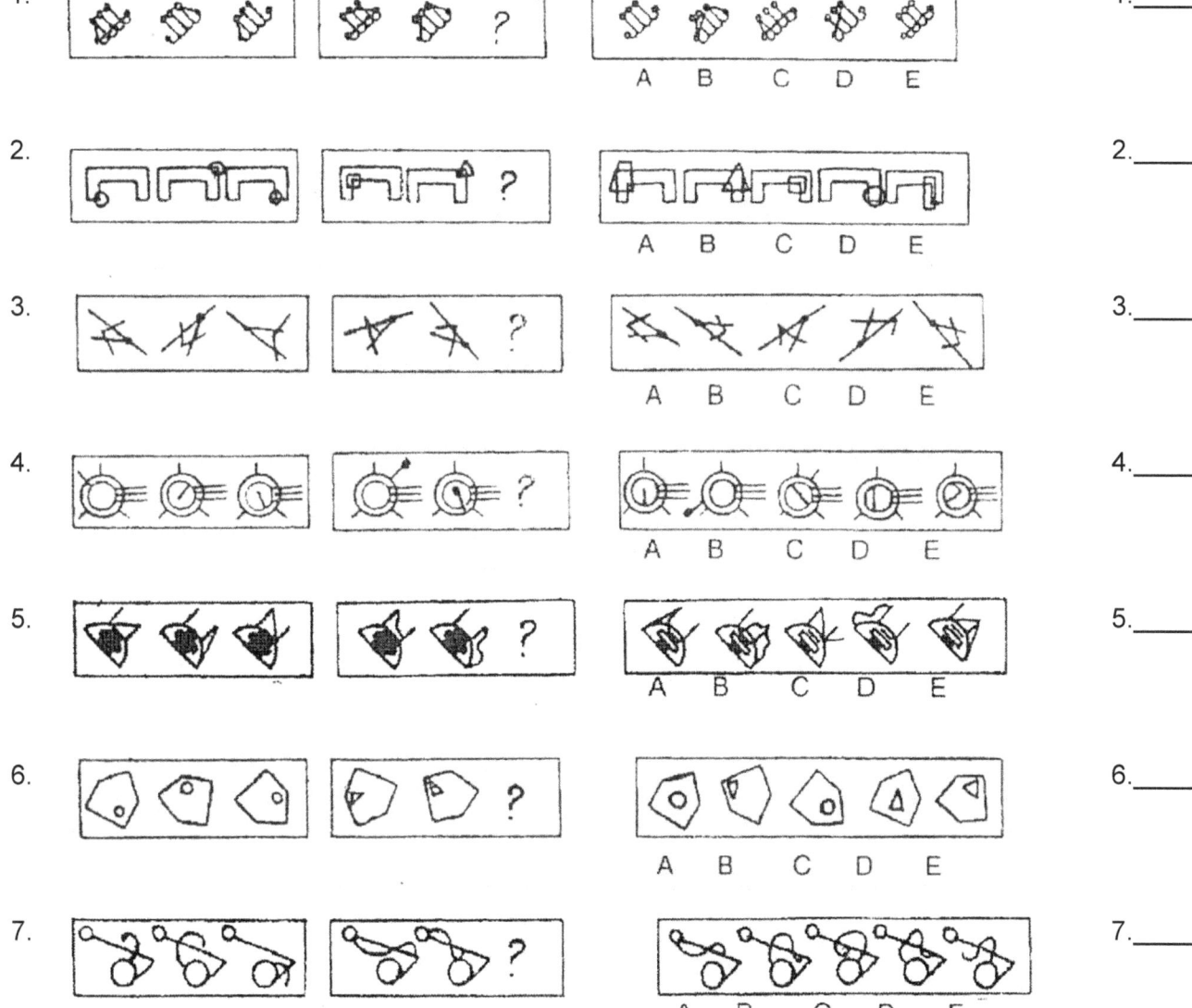

2 (#1)

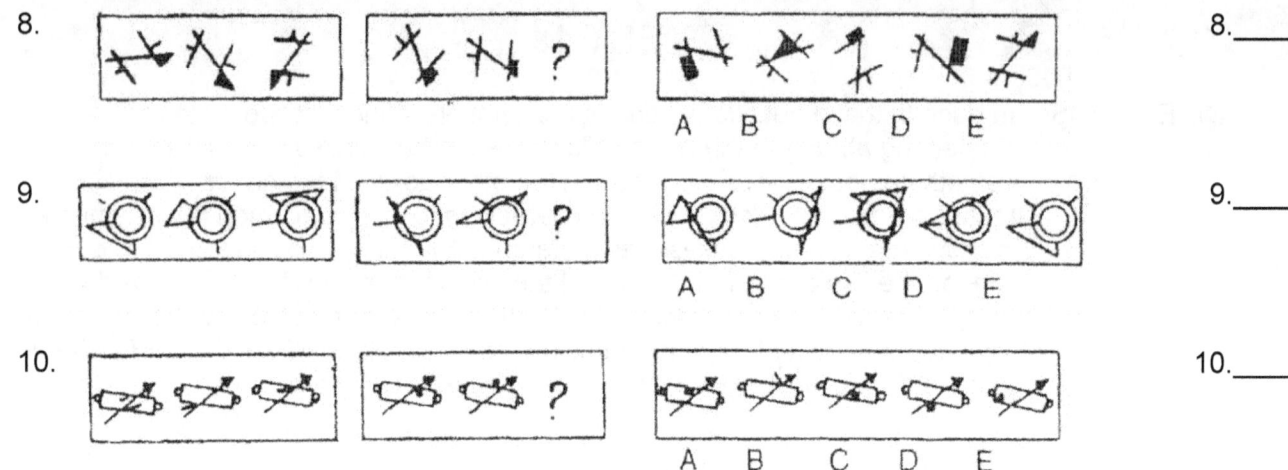

KEY (CORRECT ANSWERS)

1.	B	6.	B
2.	C	7.	A
3.	C	8.	C
4.	B	9.	B
5.	D	10.	D

TEST 2

DIRECTIONS: In each of these questions, look at the symbols in the first two boxes. Something about the three symbols in the first box makes them alike; something about the two symbols in the other box with the question mark makes them alike. Look for some characteristic that is common to all symbols in the same box, yet makes them different from the symbols in the other box. Among the five answer choices, find the symbol that can BEST be substituted for the question mark, because it is *like* the symbols in the second box, and, for the same reason, different from those in the first box. *PRINT THE LETTER OF THE CORRECT ANSWER IN THE SPACE AT THE RIGHT.*

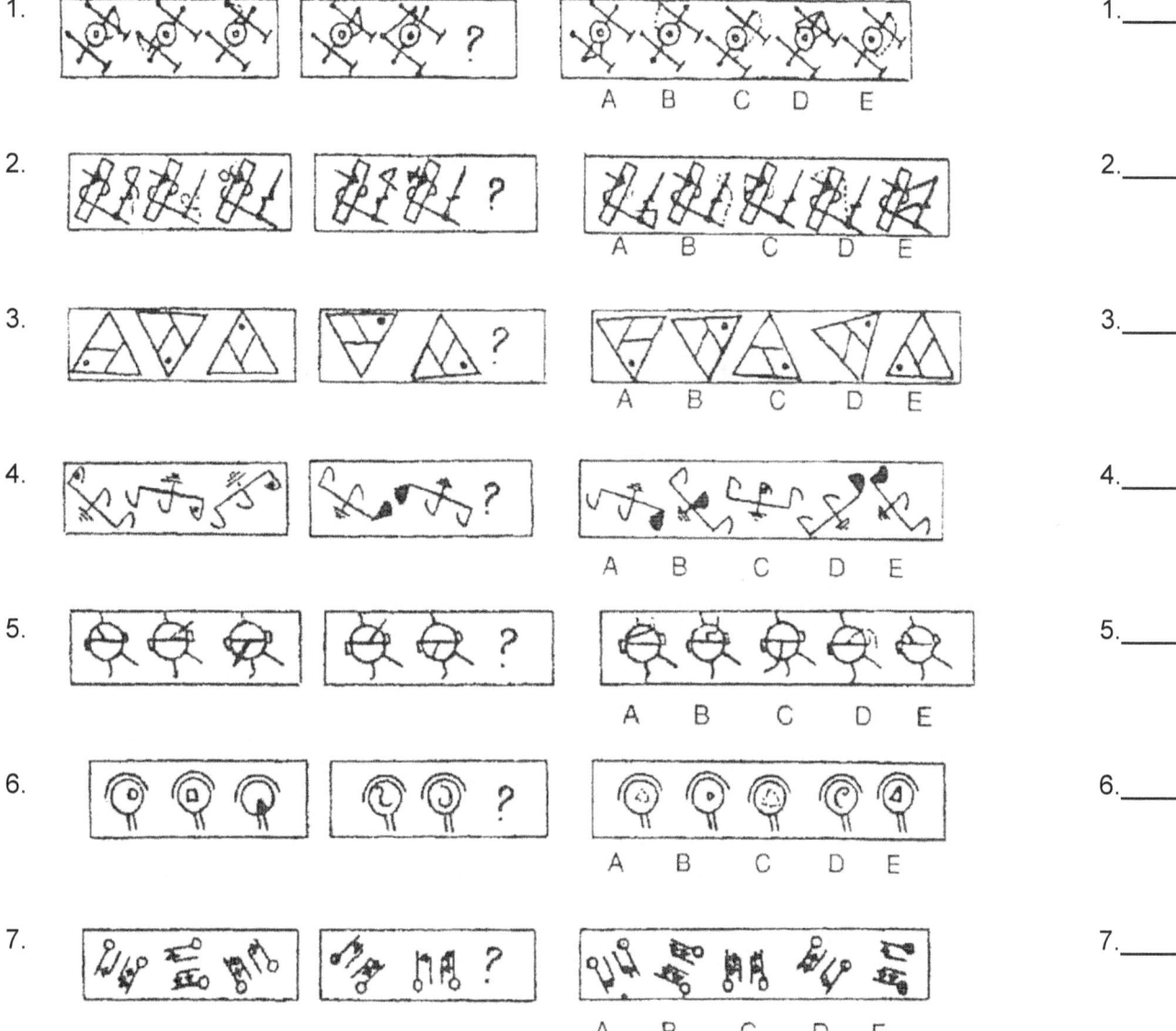

1.____

2.____

3.____

4.____

5.____

6.____

7.____

63

2 (#2)

8. 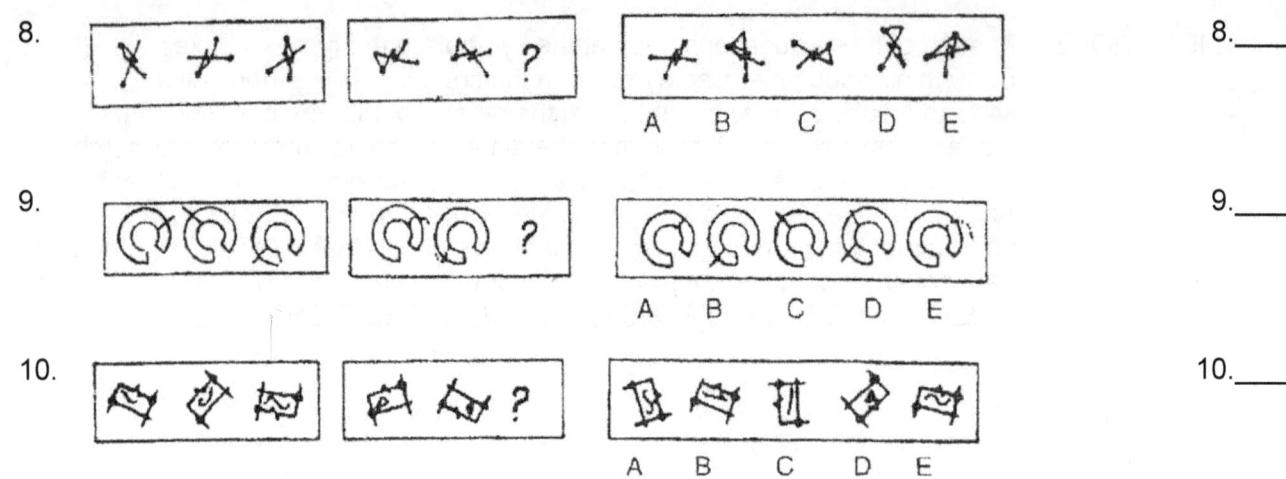 8.____

9. 9.____

10. 10.____

KEY (CORRECT ANSWERS)

1.	A	6.	D
2.	A	7.	D
3.	A	8.	C
4.	D	9.	E
5.	E	10.	D

TEST 3

DIRECTIONS: In each of these questions, look at the symbols in the first two boxes. Something about the three symbols in the first box makes them alike; something about the two symbols in the other box with the question mark makes them alike. Look for some characteristic that is common to all symbols in the same box, yet makes them different from the symbols in the other box. Among the five answer choices, find the symbol that can BEST be substituted for the question mark, because it is *like* the symbols in the second box, and, for the same reason, different from those in the first box. *PRINT THE LETTER OF THE CORRECT ANSWER IN THE SPACE AT THE RIGHT.*

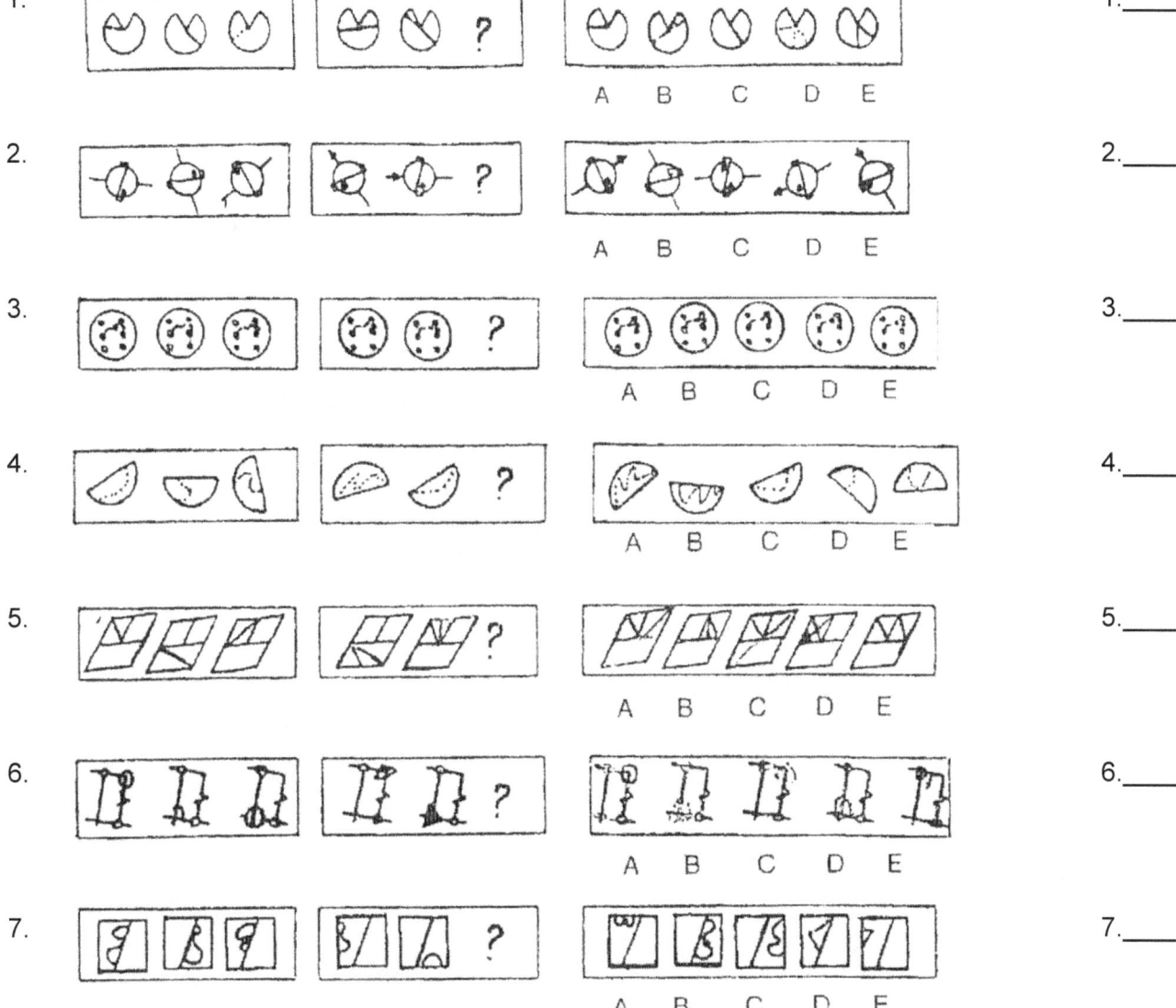

2 (#3)

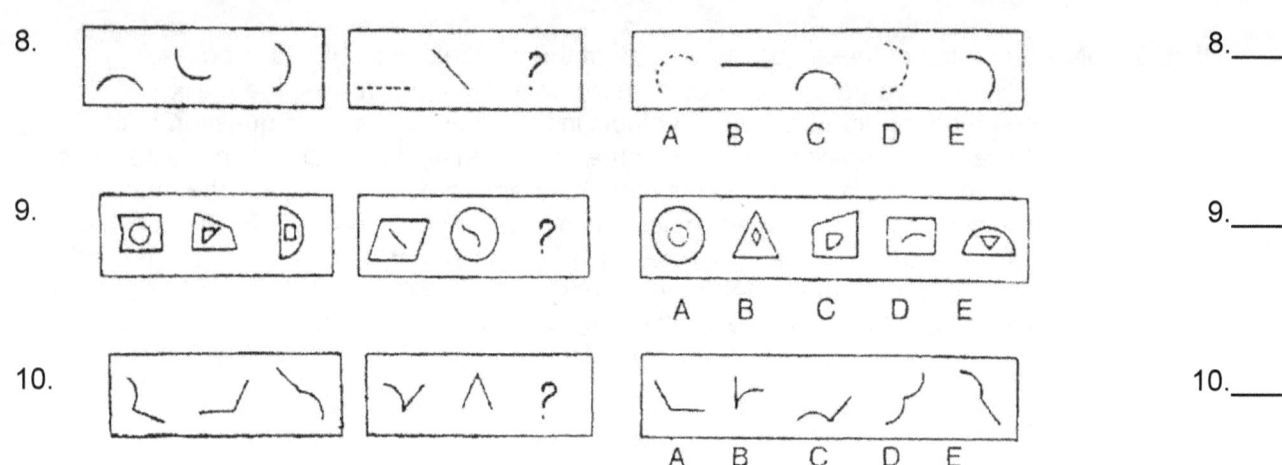

KEY (CORRECT ANSWERS)

1.	B	6.	C
2.	E	7.	C
3.	C	8.	B
4.	A	9.	D
5.	B	10.	B

ABSTRACT REASONING

COMMENTARY

The mathematical or quantitative ability of the candidate is generally measured through the form of questions and/or problems involving arithmetical reasoning, algebraic problem solving, and the interpretation of visual materials graphs, charts, tables, diagrams, maps, cartoons, and pictures.

A more recent development, which attempts to assay facets of quantitative ability not ordinarily discernible or measurable, is the nonverbal test of reasoning of the type commonly designated as the figure analogy. Figure analogies are novel and differentiated measures of non-numerical mathematics reasoning.

Since intelligence exists in many forms or phases and the theory of differential aptitudes is now firmly established in testing, other manifestations and measurements of intelligence than verbal or purely arithmetical must be identified and measured.

Classification inventory, or figure classification, involves the aptitude of form perception, i.e., the ability to perceive pertinent detail in objects or in pictorial or graphic material. It involves making visual comparisons and discriminations and discerning slight differences in shapes and shading figures and widths and lengths of lines.

One aspect of this type of nonverbal question takes the form of a *positive* requirement to find the *COMPATIBLE PATTERN* (i.e., the one that *does* belong) from among two (2) sets of figure groups. The prescription for this question-type is as follows:

A group of three drawings lettered A, B, and C, respectively, is presented, followed on the same line by five (5) numbered alternative drawings labeled 1, 2, 3, 4, and 5, respectively.

The first two (2) drawings (A, B) in each question are related in some way.

The candidate is then to decide what characteristic *each* of the figures labeled A and B has that causes them to be related, and is then to select the one alternative from the five (5) numbered figures that is related to figure C in the same way that drawing B is related to drawing A.

Leading examples of presentation are the figure analogy and the figure classification. The section that follows presents progressive and varied samplings of this type of question.

FIGURE ANALOGIES

Figure analogies are a novel and differentiated measure of non-numerical mathematics reasoning.

This question takes the form of, and, indeed, is similar to, the one-blank verbal analogy. However, pictures or drawings are used instead of words.

SAMPLE QUESTIONS AND EXPLANATIONS

DIRECTIONS: Each question in this part consists of 3 drawings lettered A,B,C, followed by 5 alternative drawings, numbered 1 to 5. The first 2 drawings in each question are related in some way. Choose the number of the alternative that is related to the third drawing in the same way that the second drawing is related to the first, and mark the appropriate space on your answer sheet.

1.

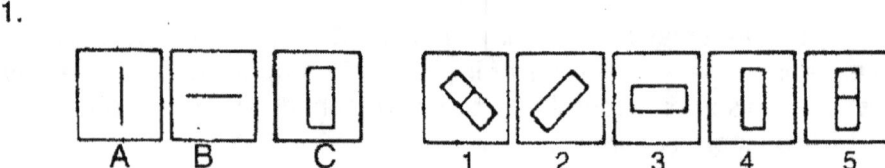

The CORRECT answer is 3. A vertical line has the same relationship to a horizontal line that a rectangle standing on its end has to a rectangle lying on its side.

2.

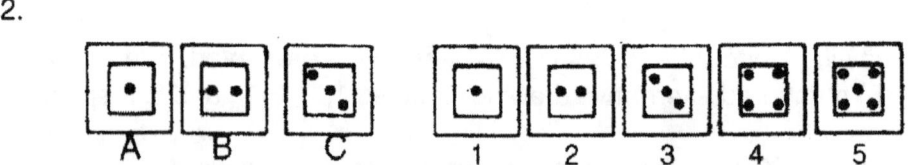

The second square has one more dot than the first square. Therefore the CORRECT answer is alternative 4, which has one more dot than the third square.

3.

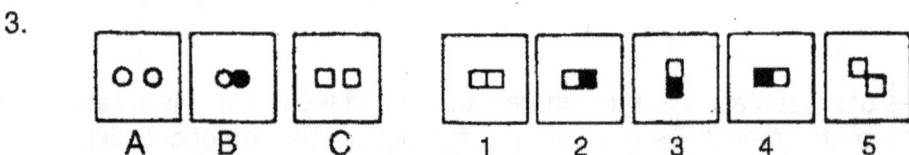

In the second drawing the circles are moved together and the circle on the right darkened. Therefore the CORRECT answer is 2, in which the squares are moved together and the right-hand square darkened.

4.

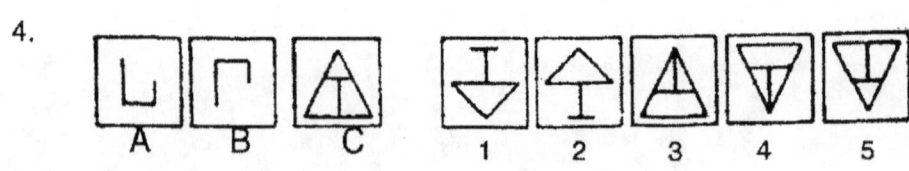

The CORRECT answer is 5. The second drawing is the inverted version of the first; alternative 5 is the inverted version of the third drawing.

5.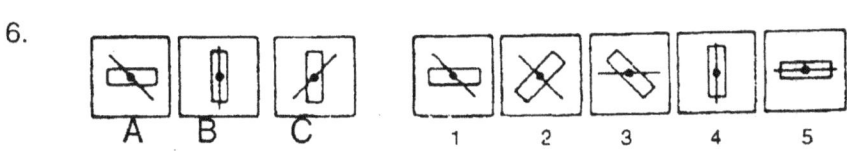

The CORRECT answer is 4. Drawing A has a small circle within a square; drawing B contains a circle completely filling the square. Drawing C has a small square within a square; in alternative 4, this small square has been magnified to its complete size within the square so that this magnified square coincides with the enclosing square, leaving the outline of only one square.

6.

The CORRECT answer is 5. Drawing A appears in a horizontal position, with a diagonal line drawn through the center dot; drawing B appears in a vertical position, with a straight line drawn through the center dot. Drawing C is similar to drawing A, except that it appears in a vertical position; drawing 5 is similar to drawing B, except that it appears in a horizontal position. Our analogy may, therefore, be verbally expressed as
A:B:C:5.

SUGGESTIONS FOR ANSWERING THE FIGURE ANALOGY QUESTION

1. In doing the actual questions, there can be little practical gain in rationalizing each answer that you attempt. What is needed is a quick and ready perceptive sense in this matter.

2. The BEST way to prepare for this type of question is to do the "Tests" in figure analogies that follow. By this method, you will gain enough functional skill to enable you to cope successfully with this type of question on the Examination.

PLEASE NOTE -- In the tests which begin on page 5, after the sample questions, the three (3) drawings are unlabeled and the answers have four (4) choices instead of five (5) labeled A, B, C and D. They are to be answered in the same way.

SAMPLE TEST

1.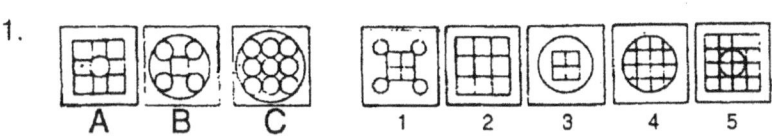

4 (#1)

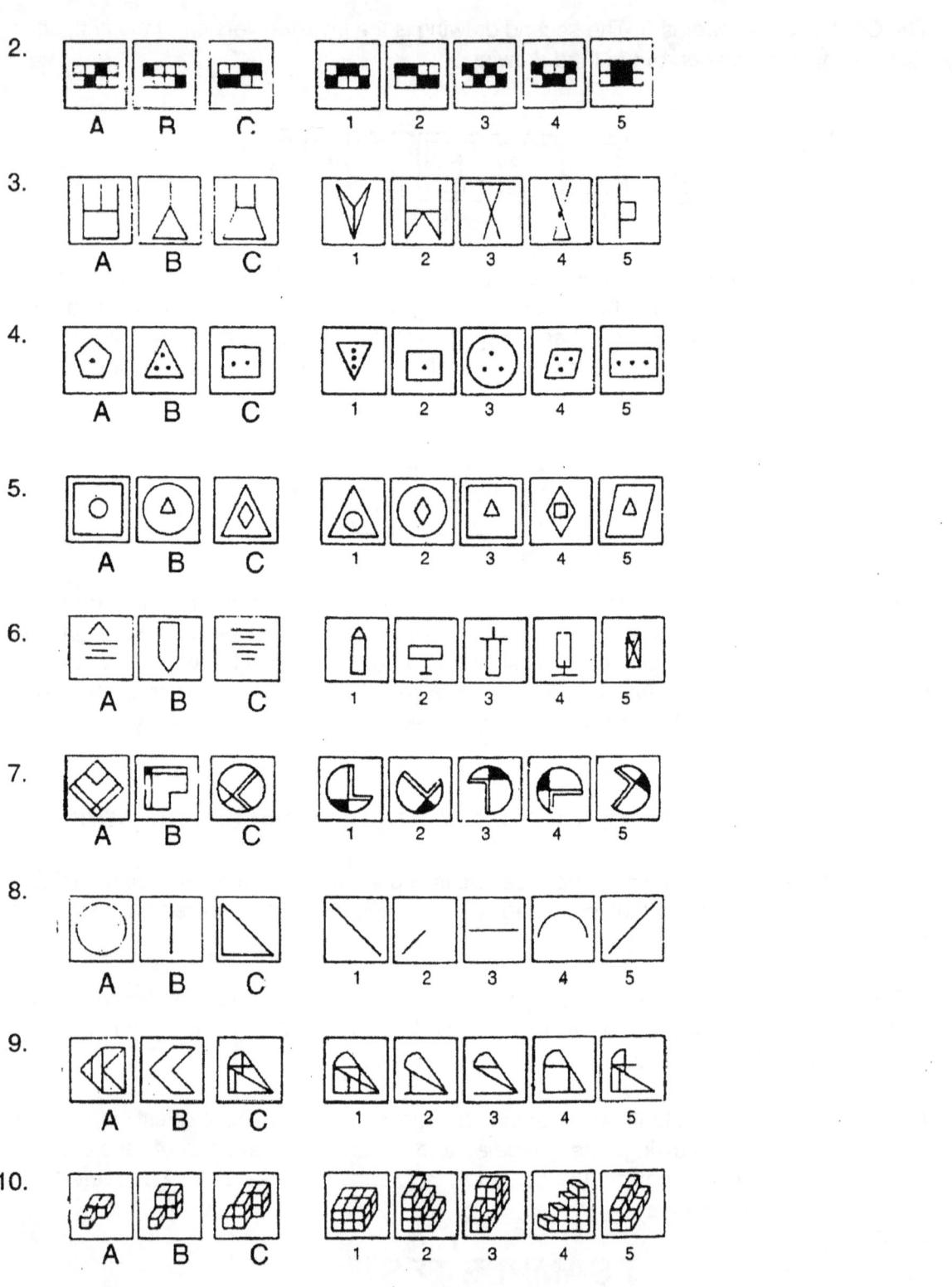

KEY (CORRECT ANSWERS)

1. 2
2. 2
3. 4
4. 1

5. 4
6. 3
7. 3
8. 2

EXPLANATION OF ANSWERS

1. In the second figure, the squares are changed to circles and the circles to squares.

2. In the second figure, the upper darkened area has moved two squares to left; the lower, two squares to right.

3. The second figure has a flat base, like the first.

4. The sum of sides and dots in the second figure equals that of the first.

5. The outside part of the second figure is the inside part of the first.

6. The second figure is constructed from the lines given in the first.

7. The second figure is obtained from the first by rotating it 135 clockwise, darkening the smaller area and deleting the larger.

8. The second figure is the bisector of the area of the first.

9. The second figure is obtained from the first by deleting all the vertical lines.

10. The second figure contains two blocks more than the first.

EXAMINATION SECTION

PROBLEM FIGURES   ANSWER FIGURES

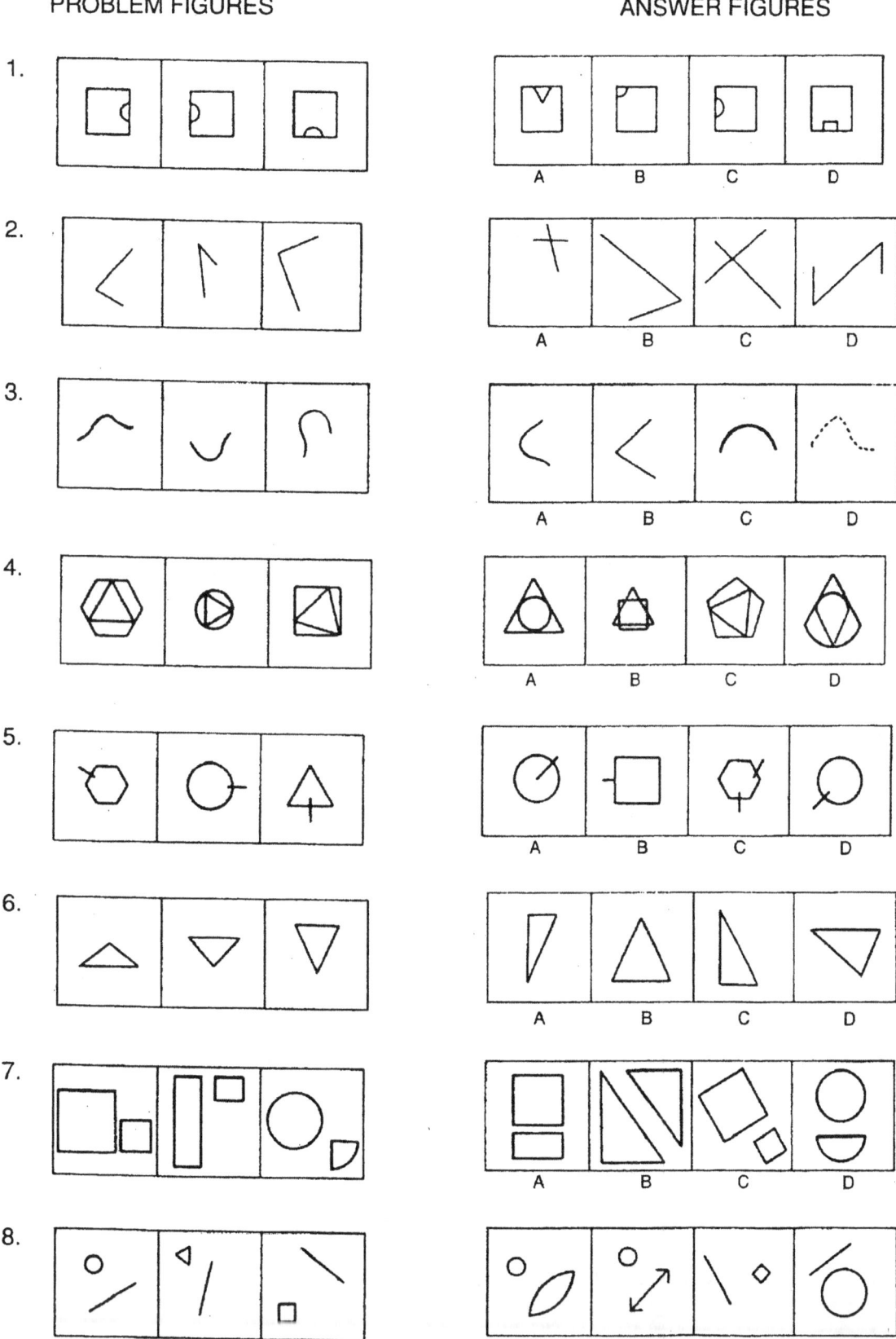

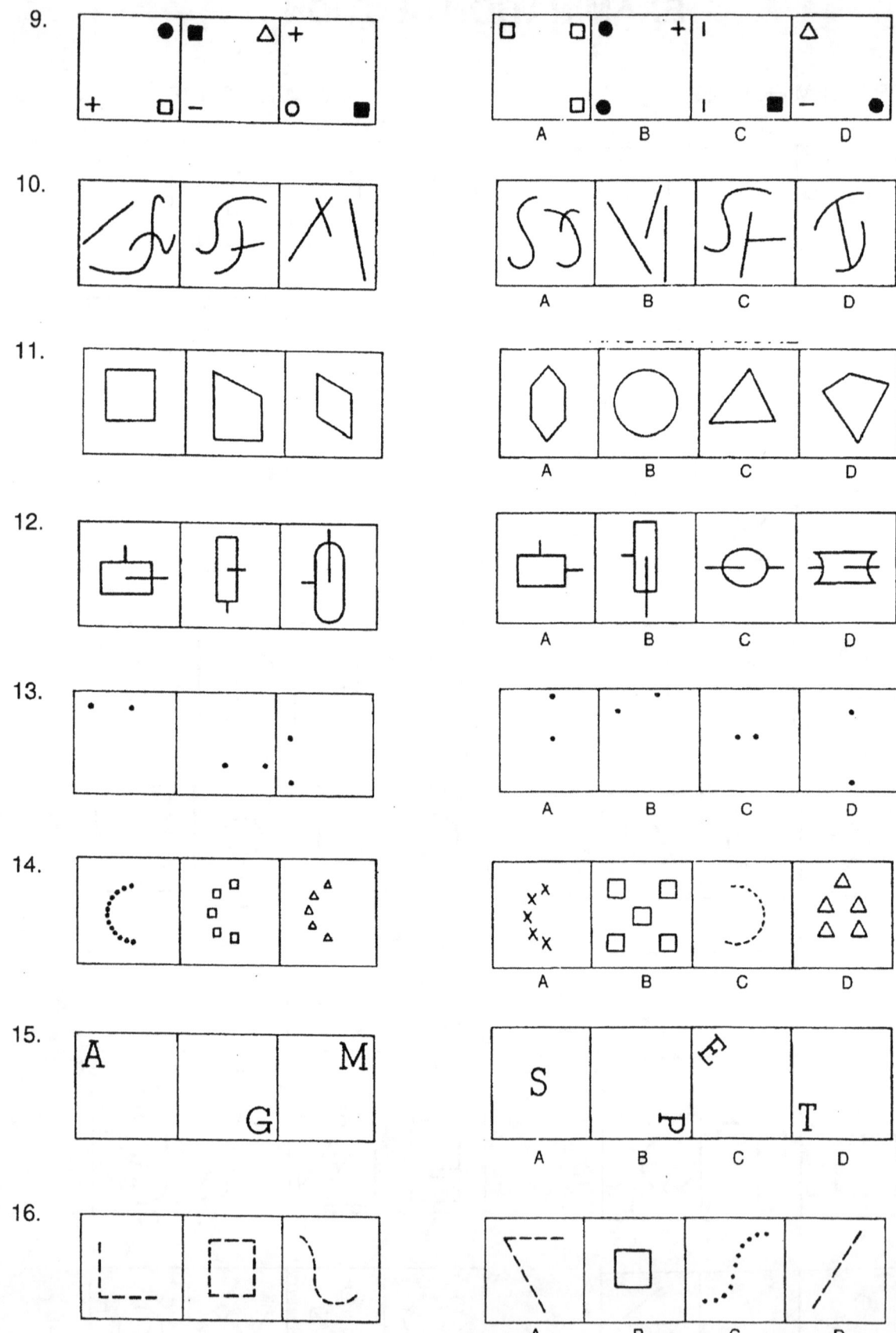

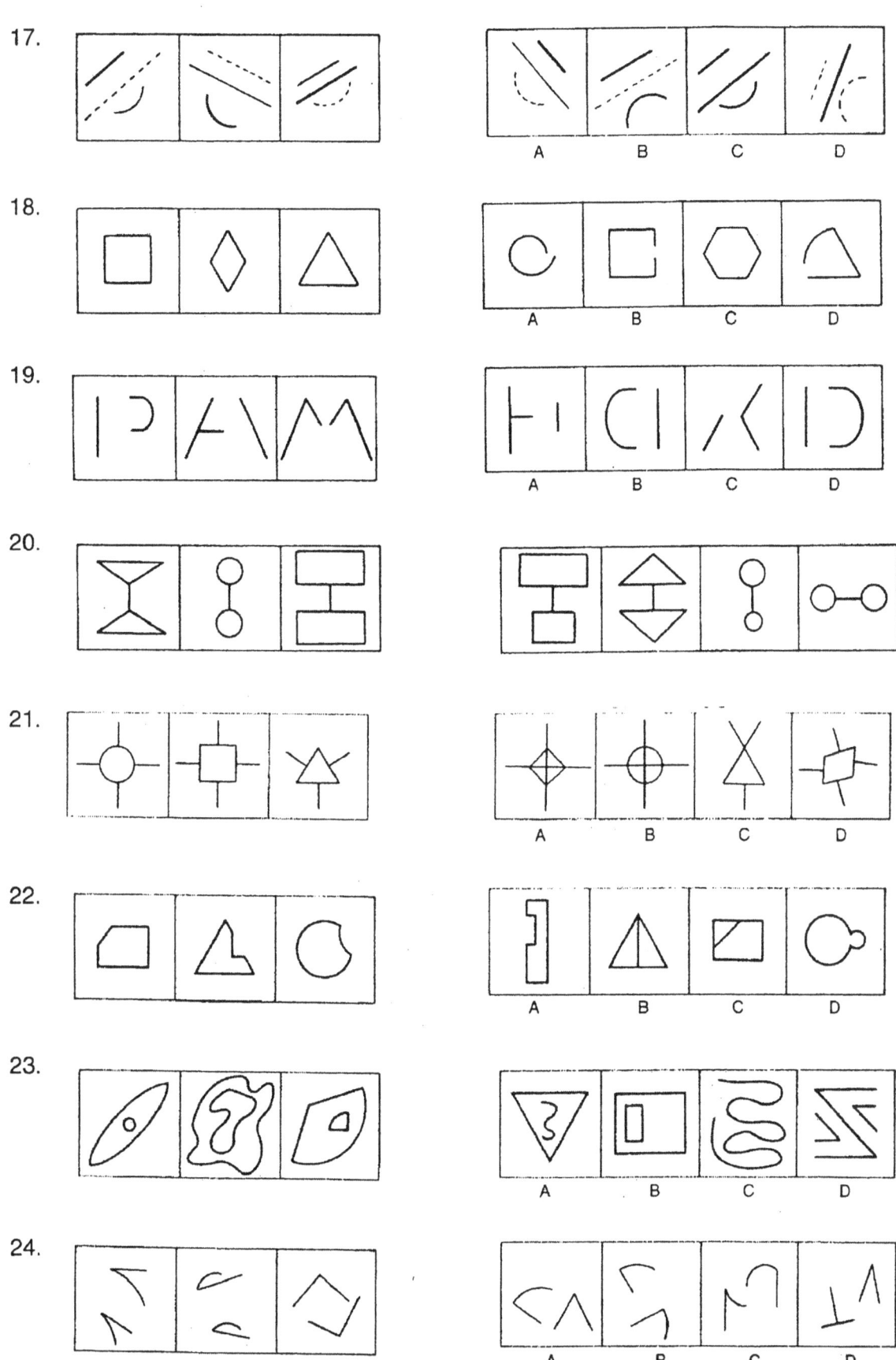

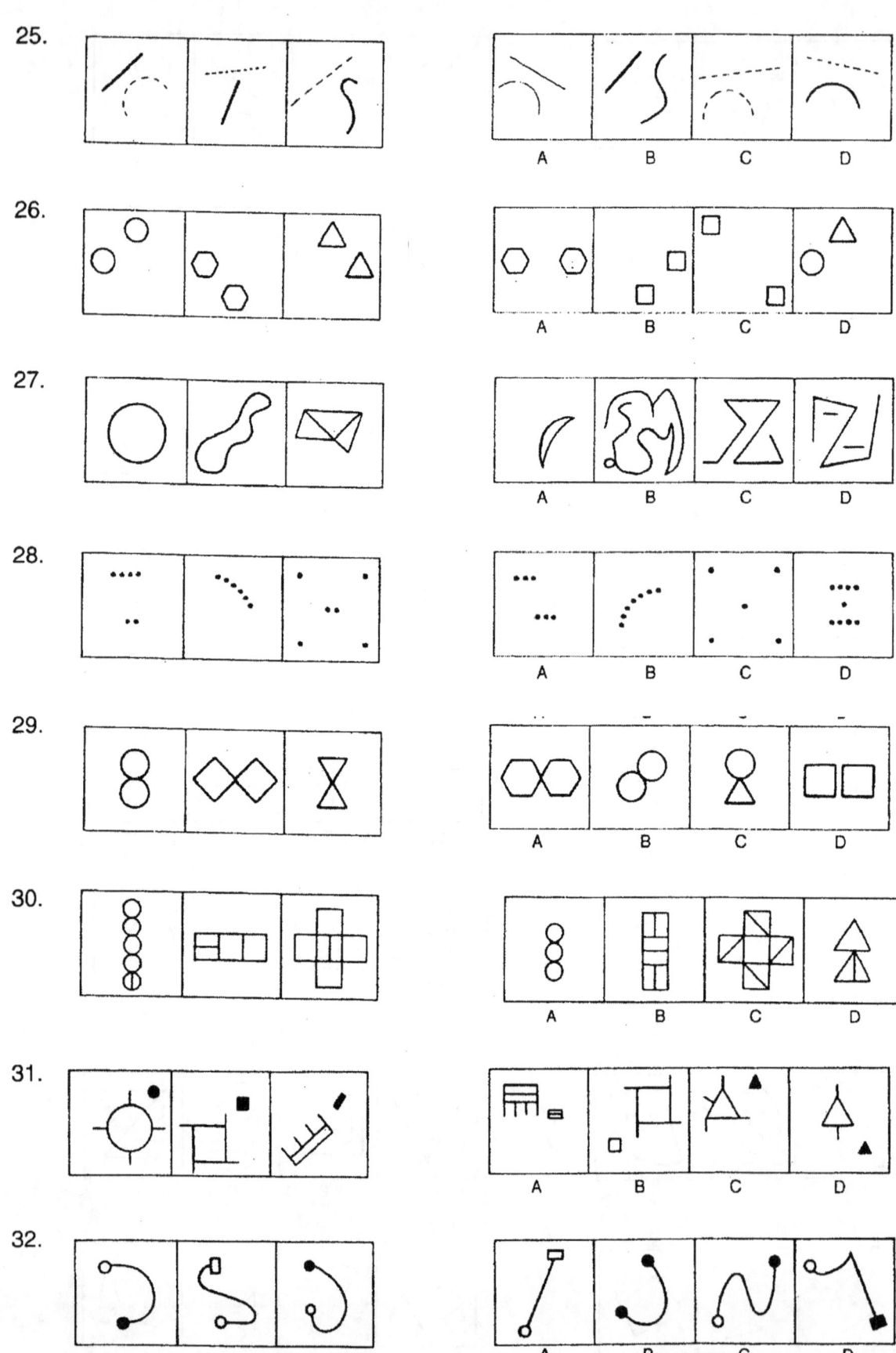

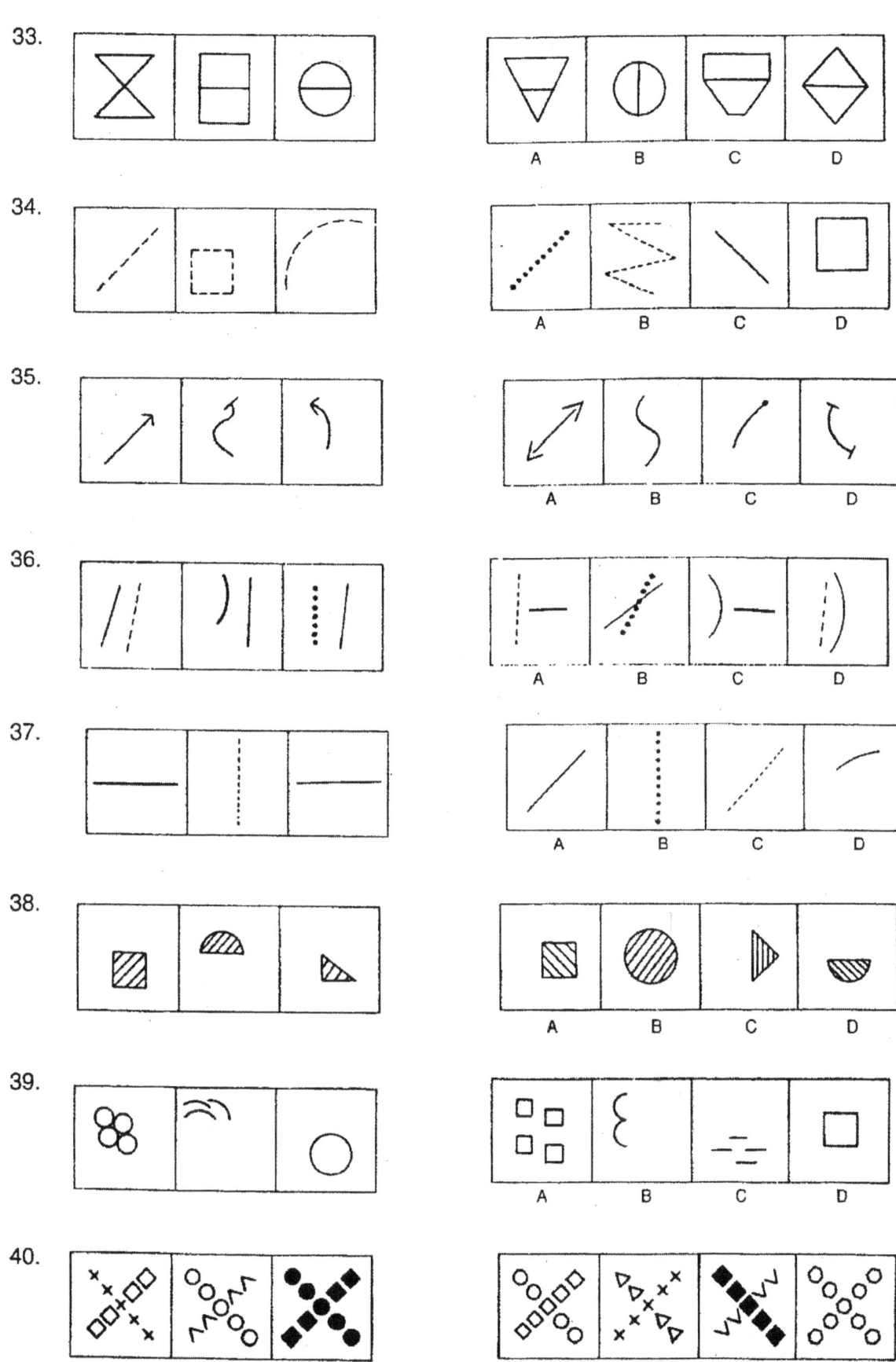

12 (#1)

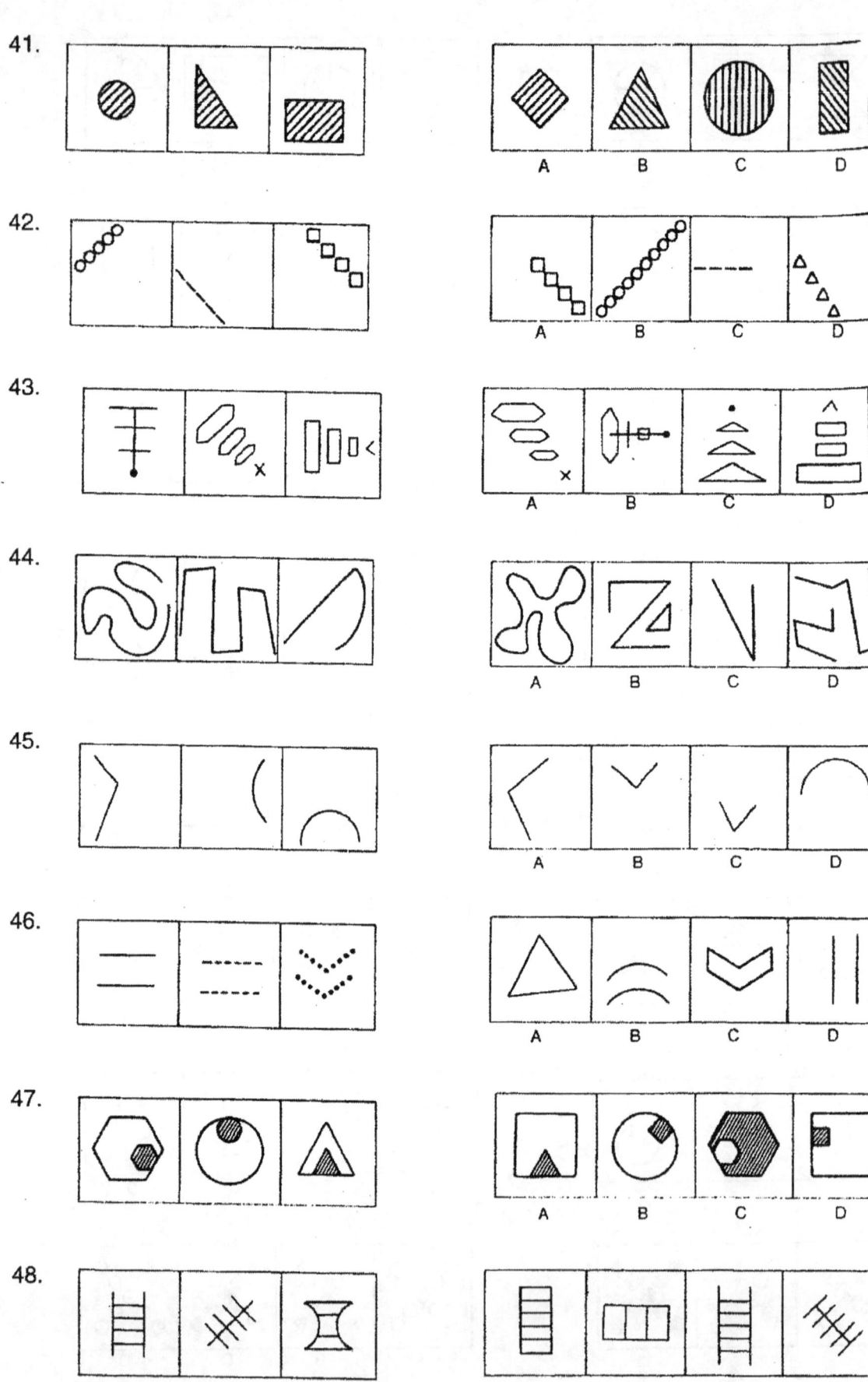

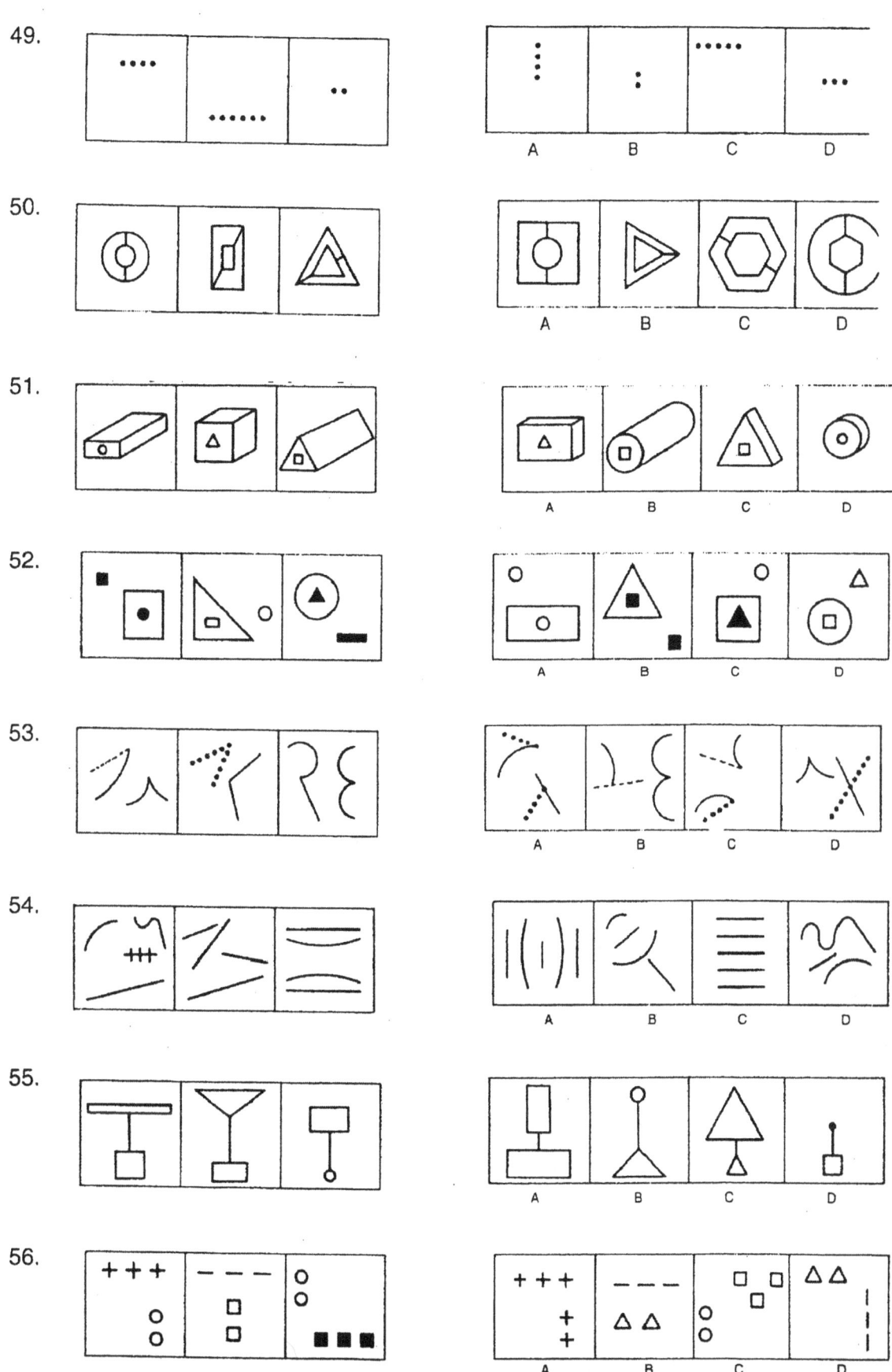

14 (#1)

57.

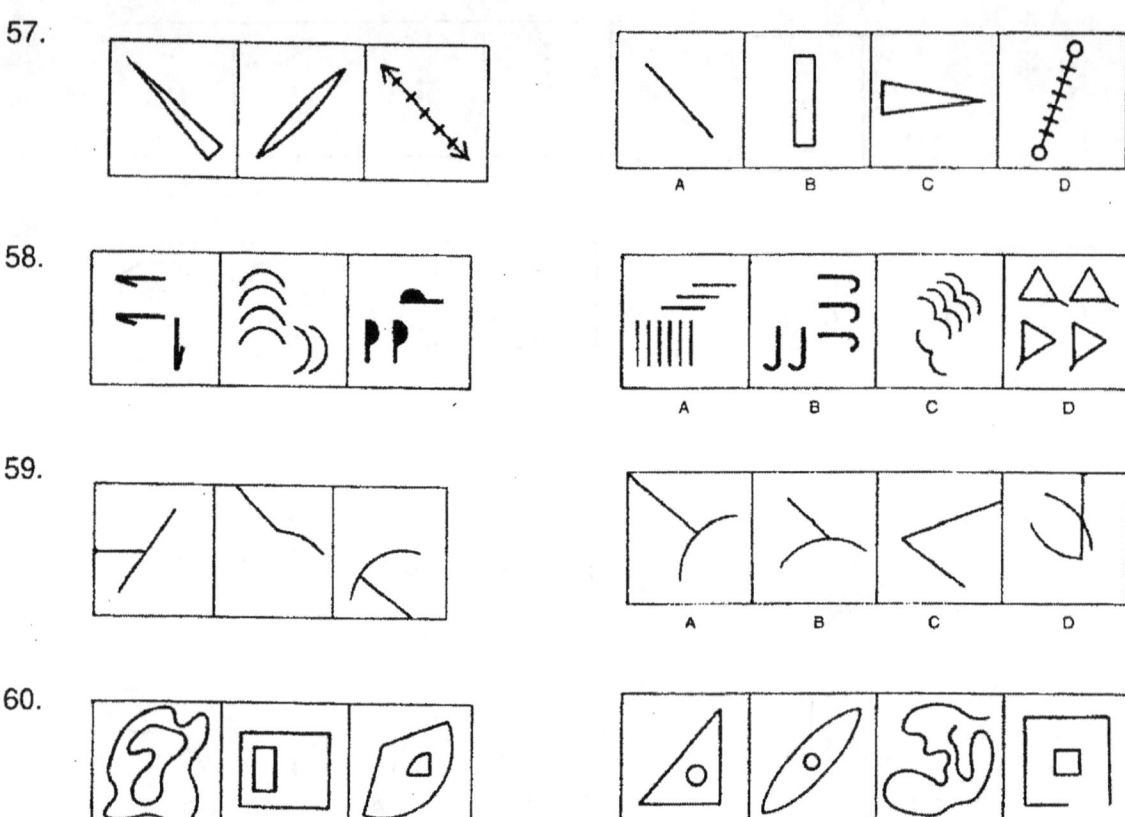

KEY (CORRECT ANSWERS)

1.	C	11.	D	21.	D	31.	C	41.	A	51.	B
2.	B	12.	B	22.	A	32.	C	42.	D	52.	D
3.	A	13.	A	23.	B	33.	D	43.	C	53.	C
4.	C	14.	A	24.	B	34.	B	44.	C	54.	B
5.	D	15.	D	25.	D	35.	C	45.	B	55.	C
6.	B	16.	A	26.	B	36.	D	46.	B	56.	D
7.	C	17.	A	27.	A	37.	B	47.	D	57.	A
8.	C	18.	C	28.	A	38.	B	48.	B	58.	A
9.	D	19.	D	29.	A	39.	B	49.	D	59.	C
10.	A	20.	B	30.	D	40.	C	50.	C	60.	B

ABSTRACT REASONING

CLASSIFICATION INVENTORY SECTION
INCOMPLETE PATTERNS (NINE FIGURES)

The tests of incomplete patterns that follow consist of items which involve the visualization of nine figures arranged in sequence.

An incomplete pattern only is given. The candidate is to select from the five-lettered choices the correct figure for the last or ninth space.

DIRECTIONS: Each item in this test consists of an incomplete pattern. The complete pattern would be made up of nine figures arranged in sequence. The candidate is to determine the correct figure for the last or ninth space from the five-lettered choices given

SAMPLE QUESTIONS AND EXPLANATIONS

QUESTIONS

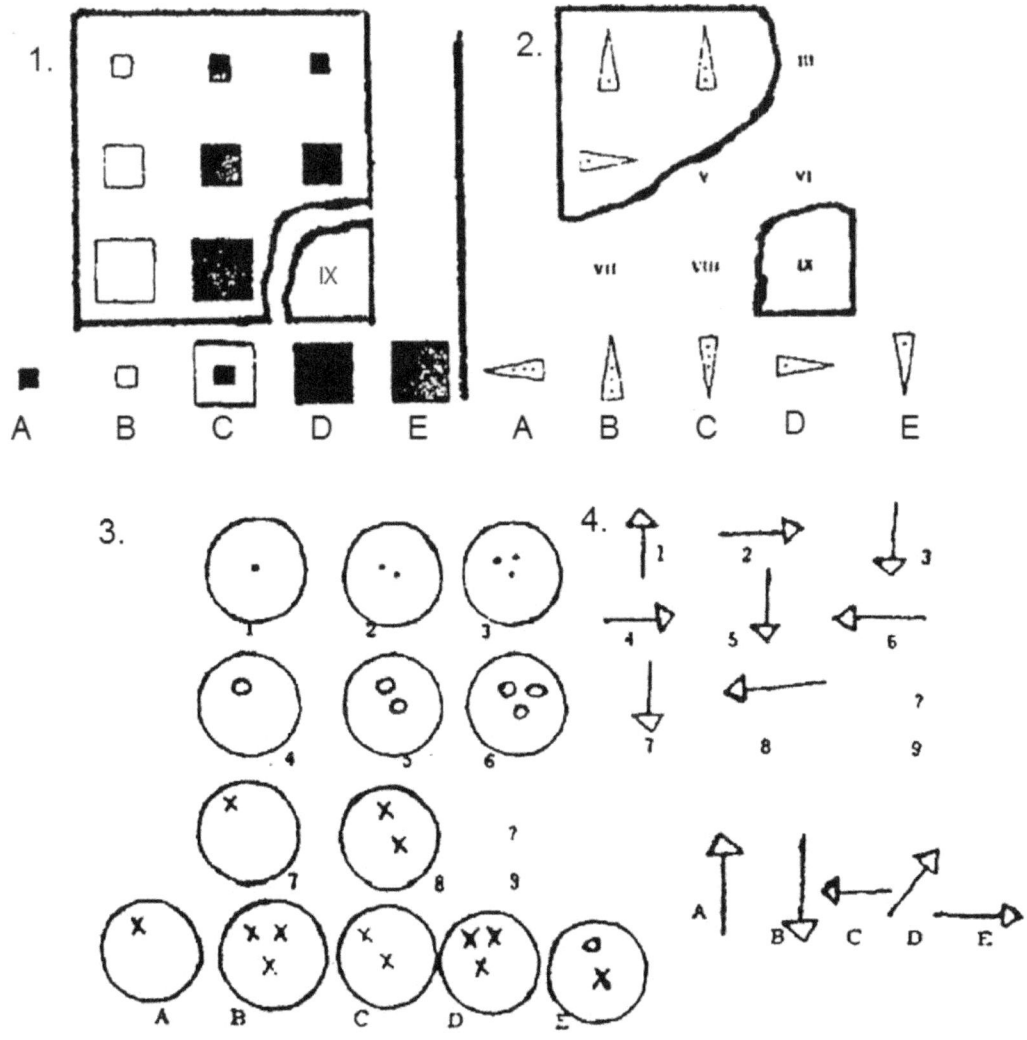

EXPLANATIONS: In Question 1, notice how the figures change as they go across each row of the pattern. They become darker. As they go down, the figures become larger. Therefore, the CORRECT figure for space IX is large is large and dark. Answer choice D is the CORRECT answer.

In Question 2, the figures acquire more dots as they go across the top row. As they go down, the point of the figure is rotated a quarter of a turn to the right. Therefore, the CORRECT answer figure for space IX has three dots and its point is directed downward toward the bottom of the page. Answer choice C is the CORRECT answer.

3. The correct answer is D. Each of the rows of circles has, exclusively, a number of ., o, or x's om ascending order. (Note that B is incorrect since the circle is larger than the given circles.)

4. The correct answer is A. Note that in row 1, two of the arrows (1,2) are turned to the right and one (3) is turned to the left. In row 2, one of the arrows (4) is turned to the right, and two (5,6) are turned to the left. In row three, two arrows are turned to the left (7,8). Therefore, one arrow (9) must be turned to the right in a similar way (answer A).

TESTS IN INCOMPLETE PATTERNS

TEST 1

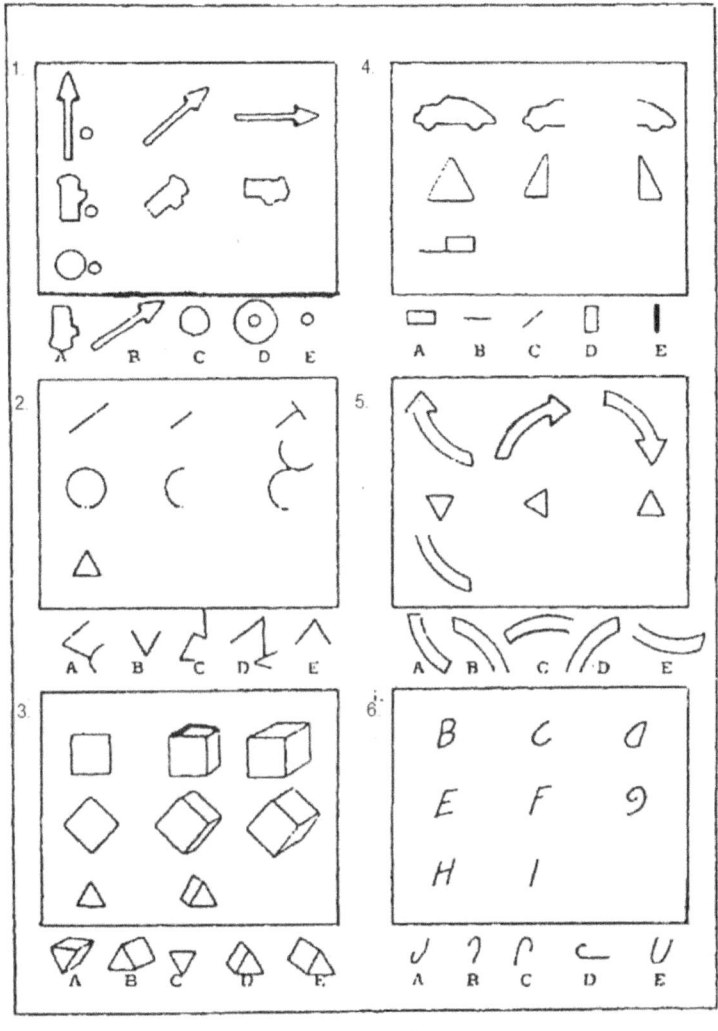

KEY (CORRECT ANSWERS)

1. C
2. C
3. E
4. A
5. B
6. C

4

TEST 2

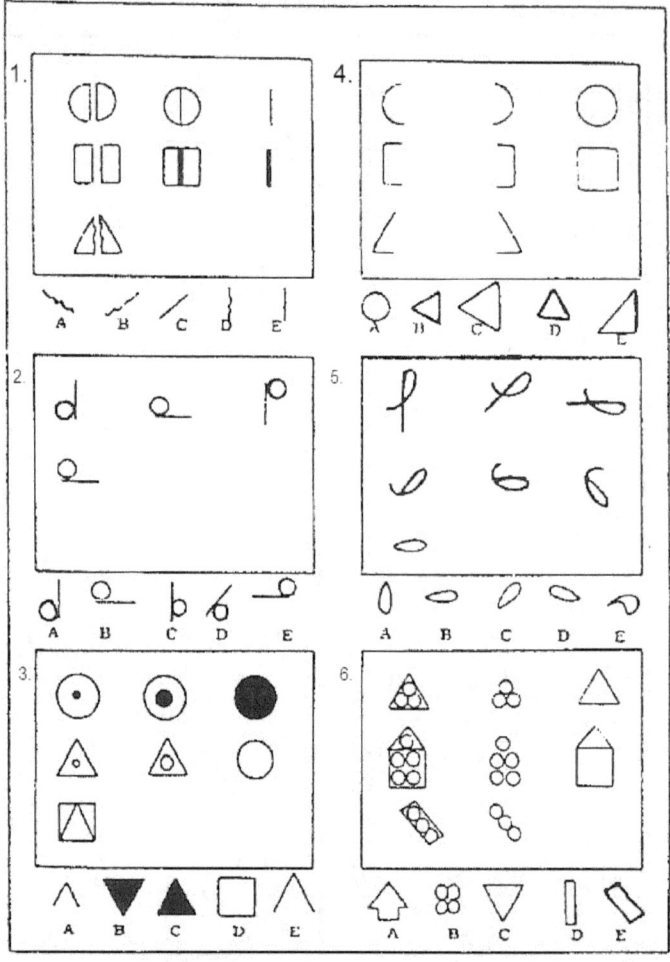

KEY (CORRECT ANSWERS)

1. D
2. A
3. E
4. C
5. A
6. E

TEST 3

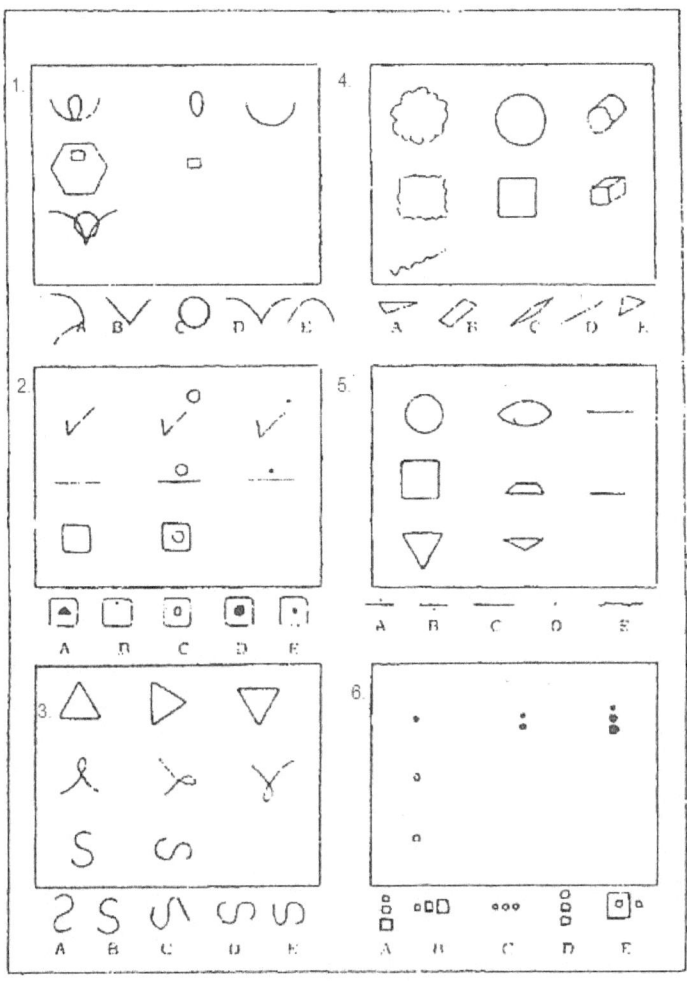

KEY (CORRECT ANSWERS)

1. D
2. E
3. B
4. C
5. C
6. A

TEST 4

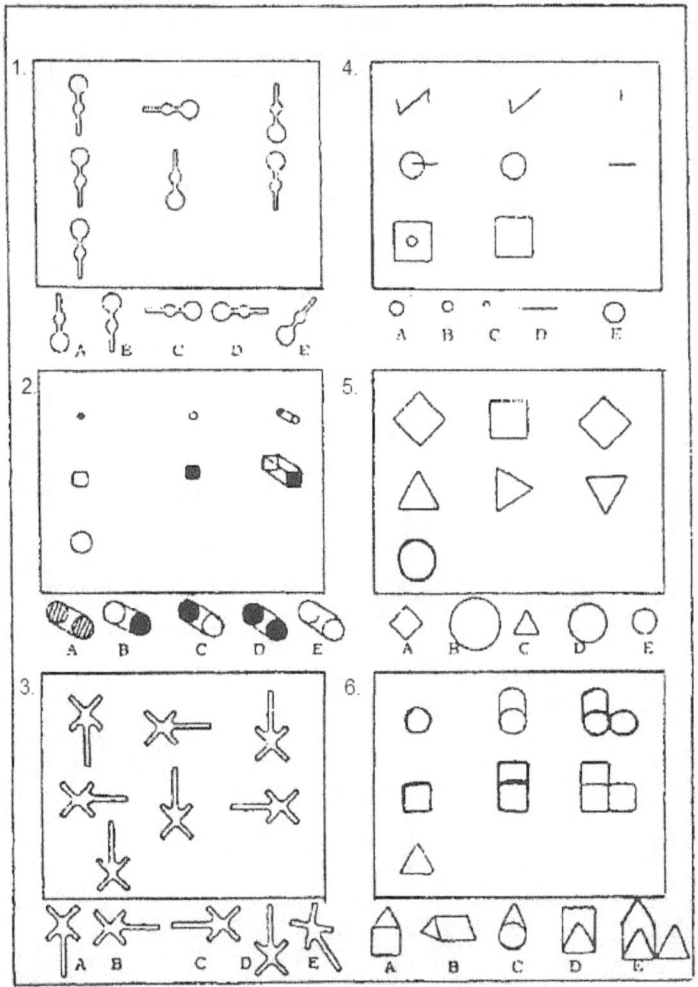

KEY (CORRECT ANSWERS)

1. A
2. B
3. A
4. B
5. D
6. E

TEST 5

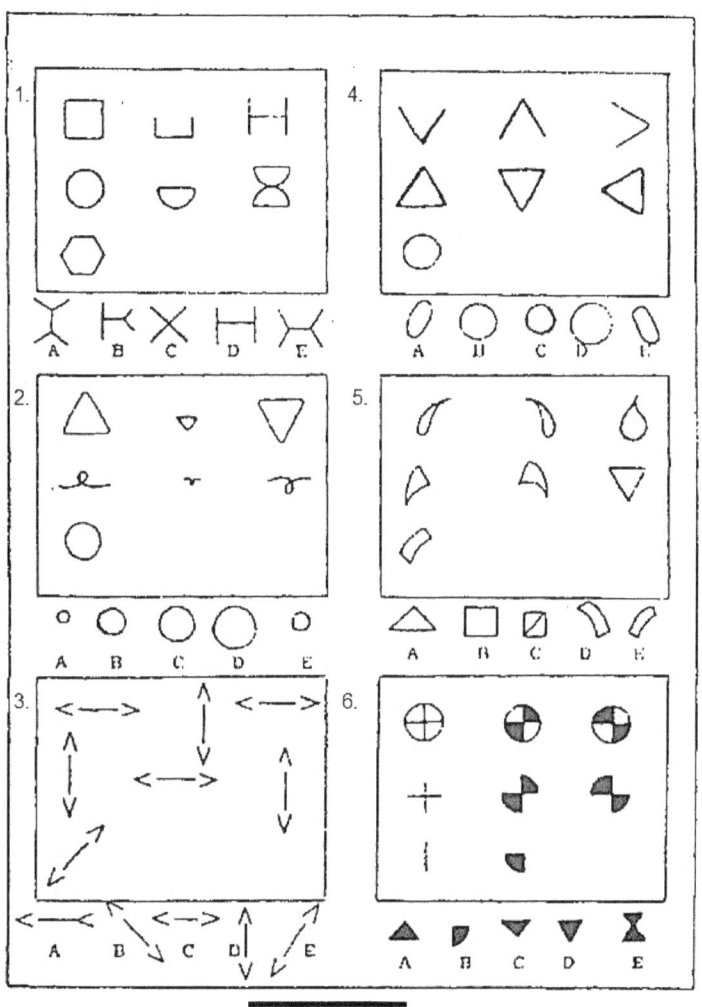

KEY (CORRECT ANSWERS)

1. E
2. C
3. E
4. B
5. B
6. B

PATTERN ANALYSIS (RIGHT SIDE ELEVATION
SAMPLE QUESTION

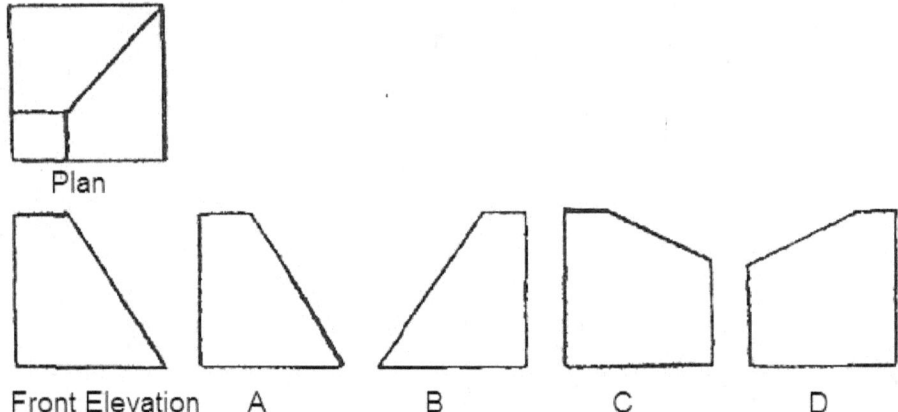

5. In the sample shown above, which figure CORRECTLY represents the right side elevation?
   1. A
   2. B
   3. C
   4. D

5.____

The correct answer is 1.

TEST 1

Questions 1-5.

DIRECTIONS: In Questions 1 through 5 which follow, the plan and front elevation of an object are shown on the left, and on the right are shown four figures, one of which, and ONLY one, represents the right side elevation. Mark your answer in the space at the right the number which represents the right side elevation.

1. A   2. B   3. C   4. D

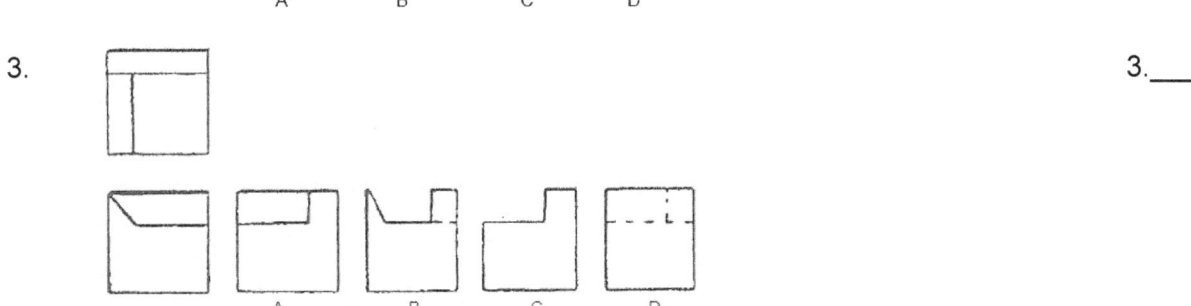

1.___

2.___

3.___

10

4.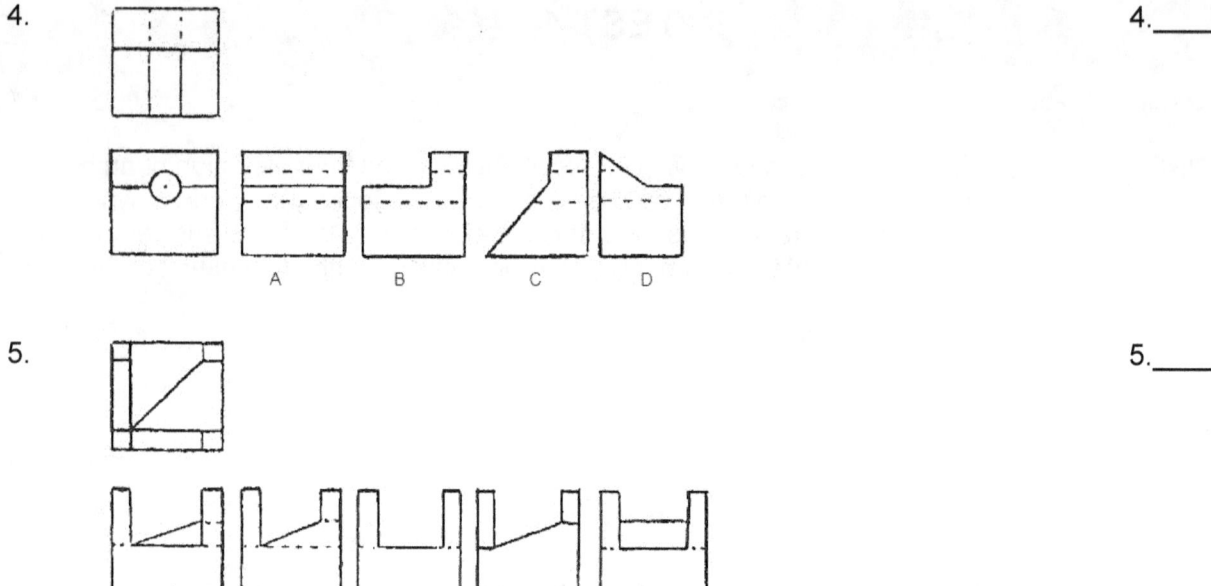

4.___

5.___

KEY (CORRECT ANSWERS)

1. 4
2. 3
3. 3
4. 2
5. 2

PATTERN ANALYSIS (END ELEVATION)

Questions 1-5.

DIRECTIONS: In each of the following groups of drawings, the top view and front elevation of an object are shown at the left. At the right are four drawings, one of which represents the end elevation of the object as seen from the right. Select the drawing which represents the CORRECT end elevation. The first group is shown as a sample ONLY.

SAMPLE QUESTION

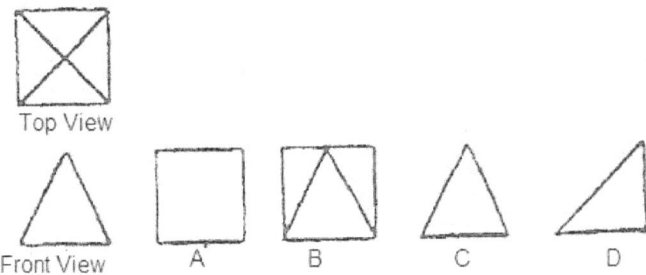

Which drawing represents the CORRECT end elevation?
1. A   2. B.   3. C   4. D

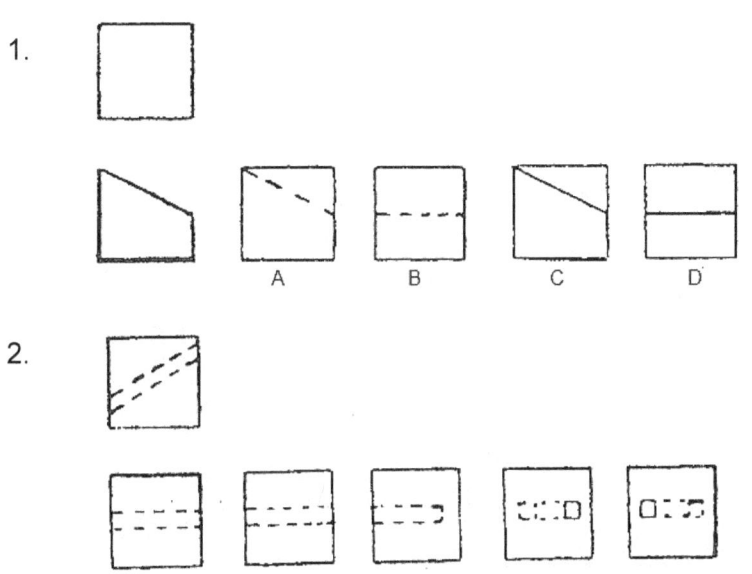

12

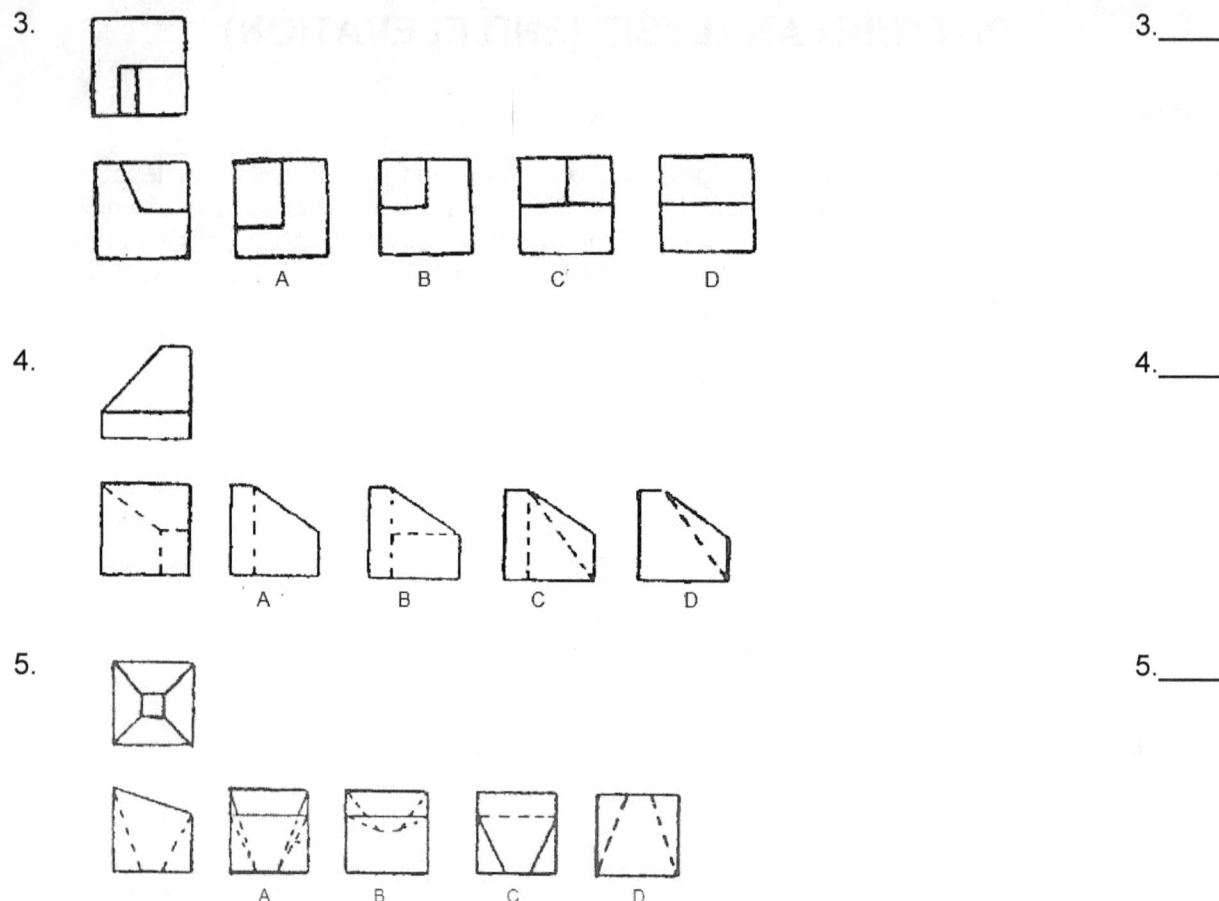

KEY (CORRECT ANSWERS)

1. 4
2. 3
3. 2
4. 1
5. 1

13

PATTERN ANALYSIS (RIGHT SIDE VIEW)

TEST 1

Questions 1-5.

DIRECTIONS: In each of Questions 1 to 5, inclusive, two views of an object are given. Of the views labeled A, B, C, and D, select the one that CORRECTLY represents the right side view of each object.

Which view represents the right side view?   1. A; 2. B; 3 C; 4. D.

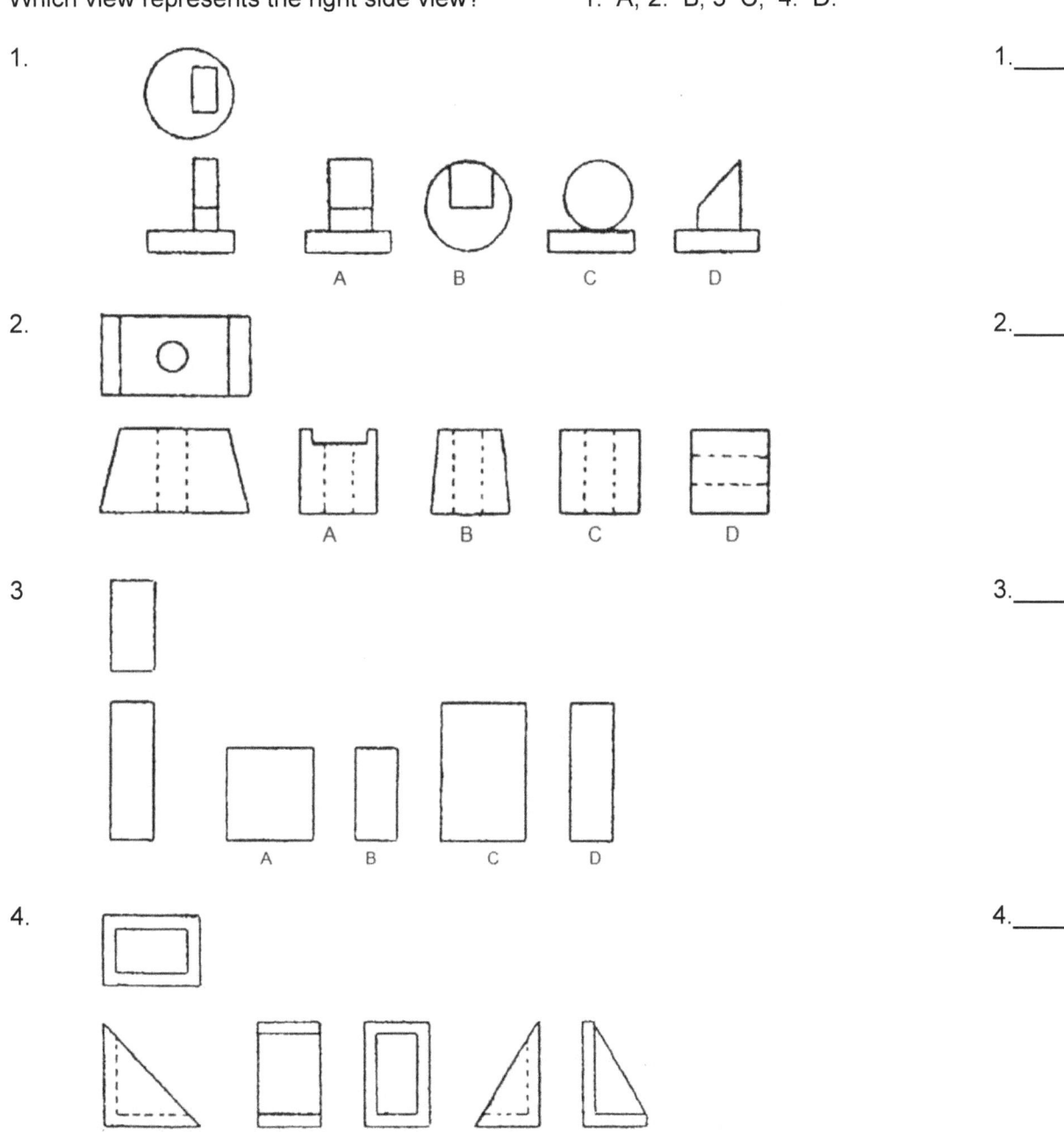

1.____

2.____

3.____

4.____

93

14

5.

   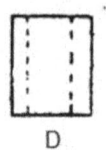
A.   B.   C.   D.

5. ____

KEY (CORRECT ANSWERS)

1. 4
2. 3
3. 3
4. 2
5. 2

15

SURVEY OF OTHER TYPES OF PATTERN ANALYSIS QUESTIONS

SOLID FIGURE TURNING

Questions 1-3.

DIRECTIONS: The following questions represent figures made up of cubes or other forms glued together. Select the ONE of the four figures lettered A, B, C, D which is the figure at the left turned in a different position and print the letter of the answer in the space at the right. (Note: You are permitted to turn over the figures, to turn them around and to turn them both over and around.)

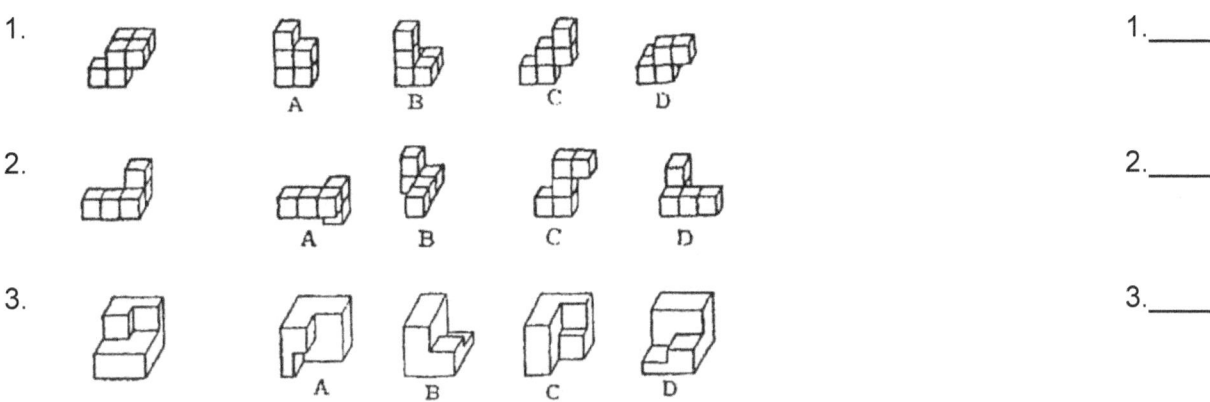

1.____

2.____

3.____

TOUCHING CUBES

Questions 4-7.

DIRECTIONS: Questions 4 and 5 are based on the group of touching cubes at the left, and Questions 6 and 7 on the group at the right.

All the cubes are exactly the same size, and there are only enough hidden cubes to support the ones you can see. The question number is on a cube in the group. You are to find how many cubes in that group touch the numbered cube. Note: A cube is considered to touch the numbered cube if ANY part, EVEN A CORNER, touches. Mark the answer in the space at the right to show how many cubes touch the numbered cube
    A.   if the answer is 1 or 6 or 11 cubes
    B.   if the answer is 2 or 7 or 12 cubes
    C.   if the answer is 3 or 8 or 13 cubes
    D.   if the answer is 4 or 9 or 14 cubes
    E.   if the answer is 5 or 10 or 15 cube

4. 4.____

5. 5.____

6. 6.____

7. 7.____

Questions 8-9.

DIRECTIONS: In each of the following questions, the drawing at the left represents a cube. There is a different design on each of the six faces of the cube. At the right are four other drawings of cubes lettered A, B, C, and D.

Select the ONE of the four which is actually the cube on the left turned to a different position and print the CORRECT answer in the space at the right. (Note: The cube at the left may have been turned over, it may have been turned may have been turned around, or it may have been turned both over and around, and faces not seen in the drawing on the left may have become visible.)

8. 6.____

A   B   C   D

9.
   A   B   C   D

7.____

CUBE COUNTING

Questions 10-15.

DIRECTIONS: In each of the following questions, count the number of boxes or cubes represented in the drawing and print the letter of the correct answer in the space at the right.

10.

   A. 16   B. 26   C. 40   D. 22

10.____

11.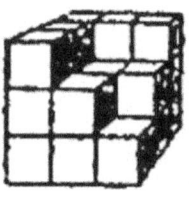

   A. 22   B. 16   C. 27   D. 24

11.____

12.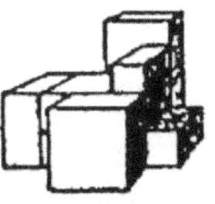

   A. 7   B. 8   C. 9   D. 10

12.____

13.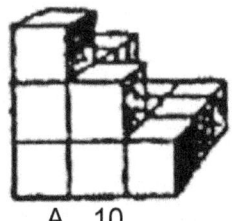

   A. 10   B. 13   C. 12   D. 14

13.____

18

14.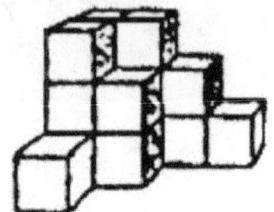

A. 15   B. 13   C. 12   D. 1-

14.____

15.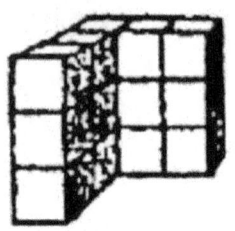

A. 16   B. 12   C. 10   D. 15

15.____

KEY (CORRECT ANSWERS)

1. D
2. B
3. D
4. C(3)
5. A(6)
6. B(7)
7. E(10)
8. B
9. A
10. C
11. A
12. B
13. .D
14. A
15. A

98

www.ingramcontent.com/pod-product-compliance
Lightning Source LLC
Chambersburg PA
CBHW082127230426
43671CB00015B/2828